Pelican Books

Deschooling Society

Ivan Illich was born in Vienna in 1926. He studied theology
and philosophy at the Gregorian University in Rome and
obtained a Ph.D. in history at the University of Salzburg.
He went to the United States in 1951, where he served as
assistant pastor in an Irish–Puerto Rican parish in New York
City. From 1956 to 1960 he was assigned as vice-rector to the
Catholic University of Puerto Rico. Illich was a co-founder
of the widely known and controversial Center for Intercultural
Documentation (CIDOC) in Cuernavaca, and from 1964
to 1976 he directed research seminars on 'Institutional Alter-
natives in a Technological Society', with special focus on Latin
America. His publications include *Celebration of Awareness*,
Limits to Medicine, Tools for Conviviality, Energy and Equity,
*Medical Nemesis, The Right to Useful Unemployment, Toward a
History of Needs, Shadow-Work, Gender* and H_2O *and the Waters
of Forgetfulness*.

Deschooling Society
Ivan Illich

Penguin Books

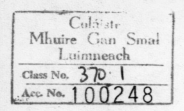
PENGUIN BOOKS

Published by the Penguin Group
27 Wrights Lane, London W8 5TZ, England
Viking Penguin Inc., 40 West 23rd Street, New York, New York 10010, USA
Penguin Books Australia Ltd, Ringwood, Victoria, Australia
Penguin Books Canada Ltd, 2801 John Street, Markham, Ontario, Canada L3R 1B4
Penguin Books (NZ) Ltd, 182–190 Wairau Road, Auckland 10, New Zealand

Penguin Books Ltd, Registered Offices: Harmondsworth, Middlesex, England

First published in the USA by Harper & Row 1971
Deschooling Society was originally published in the United
States by Harper & Row in their World Perspectives Series
(planner and editor, Ruth Nanda Anshen).
First published in Great Britain by Calder & Boyars 1971
Published by Penguin Books 1973
Reissued in Pelican Books 1976
10 9

Printed and bound in Great Britain by
Cox & Wyman Ltd, Reading

Contents

Introduction

I owe my interest in public education to Everett Reimer. Until we first met in Puerto Rico in 1958, I had never questioned the value of extending obligatory schooling to all people. Together we have come to realize that for most men the right to learn is curtailed by the obligation to attend school. The essays given at CIDOC and gathered in this book grew out of memoranda which I submitted to him, and which we discussed during 1970, the thirteenth year of our dialogue. The last chapter contains my afterthoughts on a conversation with Erich Fromm on Bachofen's *Mutterrecht*.

Since 1967 Reimer and I have met regularly at the Center for Intercultural Documentation (CIDOC) in Cuernavaca, Mexico. Valentine Borremans, the director of the Center, also joined our dialogue, and constantly urged me to test our thinking against the realities of Latin America and Africa. This book reflects her conviction that the ethos, not just the institutions, of society ought to be 'deschooled'.

Universal education through schooling is not feasible. It would be no more feasible if it were attempted by means of alternative institutions built on the style of present schools. Neither new attitudes of teachers towards their pupils nor the proliferation of educational hardware or software (in classroom or bedroom), nor finally the attempt to expand the pedagogue's responsibility until it engulfs his pupils' lifetimes will deliver universal education. The current search for new educational *funnels* must be reversed into the search for their institutional inverse: educational *webs* which heighten the opportunity for each one to transform each moment of his living into one of learning, sharing and caring. We hope to contribute concepts needed by those who conduct such counterfoil research on education – and also to those who seek alternatives to other established service industries.

On Wednesday mornings, during the spring and summer of 1970, I submitted the various parts of this book to the participants in our CIDOC programmes in Cuernavaca. Dozens of them made suggestions or provided criticisms. Many will recognize their ideas in these pages, especially Paulo Freire, Peter Berger and José María Bulnes, as well as Joseph Fitzpatrick, John Holt, Angel Quintero, Layman Allen, Fred Goodman, Gerhard Ladner, Didier Piveteau, Joel Spring, Augusto Salazar Bondy and Dennis Sullivan. Among my critics, Paul Goodman most radically obliged me to revise my thinking. Robert Silvers provided me with brilliant editorial assistance on chapters 1, 3 and 6, which have appeared in the *New York Review of Books*.

Reimer and I have decided to publish separate views of our joint research. He is working on a comprehensive and documented exposition, which will be subjected to several months of further critical appraisal and be published late in 1971 by Doubleday & Company and Penguin Education [*School is Dead*]. Dennis Sullivan, who acted as secretary at the meetings between Reimer and myself, is preparing a book which will place my argument in the context of current debate about public schooling in the United States. I offer this volume of essays now in the hope that it will provoke additional critical contributions to the sessions of a seminar on 'Alternatives in Education' planned at CIDOC in Cuernavaca for 1972 and 1973.

I intend to discuss some perplexing issues which are raised once we embrace the hypothesis that society can be deschooled; to search for criteria which may help us distinguish institutions which merit development because they support learning in a deschooled milieu; and to clarify those personal goals which would foster the advent of an Age of Leisure (*schole*) as opposed to an economy dominated by service industries.

November 1970

1 Why We Must Disestablish School

Many students, especially those who are poor, intuitively know what the schools do for them. They school them to confuse process and substance. Once these become blurred, a new logic is assumed: the more treatment there is, the better are the results; or, escalation leads to success. The pupil is thereby 'schooled' to confuse teaching with learning, grade advancement with education, a diploma with competence, and fluency with the ability to say something new. His imagination is 'schooled' to accept service in place of value. Medical treatment is mistaken for health care, social work for the improvement of community life, police protection for safety, military poise for national security, the rat race for productive work. Health, learning, dignity, independence and creative endeavour are defined as little more than the performance of the institutions which claim to serve these ends, and their improvement is made to depend on allocating more resources to the management of hospitals, schools and other agencies in question.

In these essays, I will show that the institutionalization of values leads inevitably to physical pollution, social polarization and psychological impotence: three dimensions in a process of global degradation and modernized misery. I will explain how this process of degradation is accelerated when non-material needs are transformed into demands for commodities; when health, education, personal mobility, welfare or psychological healing are defined as the result of services or 'treatments'. I do this because I believe that most of the research now going on about the future tends to advocate further increases in the institutionalization of values and that we must define conditions which would permit precisely the contrary to happen. We need research on the possible use of technology to create institutions which serve personal, creative and autonomous interaction and the emergence of values which cannot be substantially controlled by technocrats. We need counterfoil research to current futurology.

I want to raise the general question of the mutual definition of man's nature and the nature of modern institutions which characterizes our world view and language. To do so, I have chosen the school as my paradigm, and I therefore deal only indirectly with other bureaucratic agencies of the corporate state: the consumer-family, the party, the army, the Church, the media. My analysis of the hidden curriculum of school should make it evident that public education would profit from the deschooling of society, just as family life, politics, security, faith and communication would profit from an analogous process.

I begin my analysis, in this first essay, by trying to convey what the deschooling of a schooled society might mean. In this context, it should be easier to understand my choice of the five specific aspects relevant to this process with which I deal in the subsequent chapters.

Not only education but social reality itself has become schooled. It costs roughly the same to school both rich and poor in the same dependency. The yearly expenditure per pupil in the slums and in the rich suburbs of any one of twenty US cities lies in the same range – and sometimes is favourable to the poor.* Rich and poor alike depend on schools and hospitals which guide their lives, form their world view, and define for them what is legitimate and what is not. Both view doctoring oneself as irresponsible, learning on one's own as unreliable, and community organization, when not paid for by those in authority, as a form of aggression or subversion. For both groups the reliance on institutional treatment renders independent accomplishment suspect. The progressive underdevelopment of self- and community-reliance is even more typical in Westchester than it is in the north-east of Brazil. Everywhere not only education but society as a whole needs 'deschooling'.

Welfare bureaucracies claim a professional, political and finan-

*Penrose B. Jackson, *Trends in Elementary and Secondary Education Expenditures; Central City and Suburban Comparisons 1965 to 1968*, US Office of Education, Office of Program and Planning Evaluation, June 1969.

cial monopoly over the social imagination, setting standards of
what is valuable and what is feasible. This monopoly is at the
root of the modernization of poverty. Every simple need to which
an institutional answer is found permits the invention of a new
class of poor and a new definition of poverty. Ten years ago in
Mexico it was the normal thing to be born and to die in one's
own home and to be buried by one's friends. Only the soul's
needs were taken care of by the institutional church. Now to
begin and end life at home become signs either of poverty or of
special privilege. Dying and death have come under the institutional management of doctors and undertakers.

Once basic needs have been translated by a society into demands for scientifically produced commodities, poverty is defined by standards which the technocrats can change at will.
Poverty then refers to those who have fallen behind an adver-
tised ideal of consumption in some important respect. In Mexico the poor are those who lack three years of schooling, and in
New York they are those who lack twelve.

The poor have always been socially powerless. The increasing
reliance on institutional care adds a new dimension to their help-
lessness: psychological impotence, the inability to fend for themselves. Peasants on the high plateau of the Andes are exploited
by the landlord and the merchant – once they settle in Lima they
are, in addition, dependent on political bosses, and disabled by
their lack of schooling. Modernized poverty combines the lack
of power over circumstances with a loss of personal potency.
This modernization of poverty is a world-wide phenomenon, and
lies at the root of contemporary underdevelopment. Of course it
appears under different guises in rich and in poor countries.

It is probably most intensely felt in US cities. Nowhere else is
poverty treated at greater cost. Nowhere else does the treatment
of poverty produce so much dependence, anger, frustration and
further demands. And nowhere else should it be so evident that
poverty – once it has become modernized – has become resistant
to treatment with dollars alone and requires an institutional
revolution.

Today in the United States the black and even the migrant
can aspire to a level of professional treatment which would have
been unthinkable two generations ago, and which seems

grotesque to most people in the Third World. For instance, the US poor can count on a truant officer to return their children to school until they reach seventeen, or on a doctor to assign them to a hospital bed which costs sixty dollars per day – the equivalent of three months' income for a majority of the people in the world. But such care only makes them dependent on more treatment, and renders them increasingly incapable of organizing their own lives around their own experiences and resources within their own communities.

The poor in the United States are in a unique position to speak about the predicament which threatens all the poor in a modernizing world. They are making the discovery that no amount of dollars can remove the inherent destructiveness of welfare institutions, once the professional hierarchies of these institutions have convinced society that their ministrations are morally necessary. The poor in the US inner city can demonstrate from their own experience the fallacy on which social legislation in a 'schooled' society is built.

Supreme Court Justice William O. Douglas observed that 'the only way to establish an institution is to finance it'. The corollary is also true. Only by channelling dollars away from the institutions which now treat health, education and welfare can the further impoverishment resulting from their disabling side-effects be stopped.

This must be kept in mind when we evaluate federal aid programmes. As a case in point, between 1965 and 1968 over three thousand million dollars were spent in US schools to offset the disadvantages of about six million children. The programme is known as Title One. It is the most expensive compensatory programme ever attempted anywhere in education, yet no significant improvement can be detected in the learning of these 'disadvantaged' children. Compared with their classmates from middle-income homes, they have fallen further behind. Moreover, in the course of this programme, professionals discovered an additional ten million children labouring under economic and educational handicaps. More reasons for claiming more federal funds are now at hand.

This total failure to improve the education of the poor despite more costly treatment can be explained in three ways:

1. Three thousand million dollars are insufficient to improve the performance of six million children by a measurable amount; or

2. The money was incompetently spent: different curricula, better administration, further concentration of the funds on the poor child, and more research are needed and would do the trick; or

3. Educational disadvantage cannot be cured by relying on education within the school.

The first is certainly true so long as the money has been spent through the school budget. The money indeed went to the schools which contained most of the disadvantaged children, but it was not spent on the poor children themselves. These children for whom the money was intended comprised only about half of those who were attending the schools that added the federal subsidies to their budgets. Thus the money was spent for custodial care, indoctrination and the selection of social roles, as well as education, all of which functions are inextricably mingled in the physical plants, curricula, teachers, administrators and other key components of these schools, and, therefore, in their budgets.

The added funds enabled schools to cater disproportionately to the satisfaction of the relatively richer children who were 'disadvantaged' by having to attend school in the company of the poor. At best a small fraction of each dollar intended to remedy a poor child's disadvantages in learning could reach the child through the school budget.

It might be equally true that the money was incompetently spent. But even unusual incompetence cannot beat that of the school system. Schools by their very structure resist the concentration of privilege on those otherwise disadvantaged. Special curricula, separate classes or longer hours only constitute more discrimination at a higher cost.

Taxpayers are not yet accustomed to permitting three thousand million dollars to vanish from the Department of Health, Education and Welfare as if it were the Pentagon. The present Administration may believe that it can afford the wrath of educators. Middle-class Americans have nothing to lose if the programme is cut. Poor parents think they do, but, even more, they are demanding a control of the funds meant for their children. A logical way of cutting the budget and, one hopes, of increasing benefits is a system of tuition grants such as that proposed by Milton Friedman and others. Funds would be channelled to the beneficiary, enabling him to buy his share of the schooling of his choice. If such credit were limited to purchases which fit into a school curriculum, it would tend to provide greater equality of treatment, but would not thereby increase the equality of social claims.

It should be obvious that even with schools of equal quality a poor child can seldom catch up with a rich one. Even if they attend equal schools and begin at the same age, poor children lack most of the educational opportunities which are casually available to the middle-class child. These advantages range from conversation and books in the home to vacation travel and a different sense of oneself, and apply, for the child who enjoys them, both in and out of school. So the poorer student will generally fall behind so long as he depends on school for advancement or learning. The poor need funds to enable them to learn, not to get certified for the treatment of their alleged disproportionate deficiencies.

All this is true in poor nations as well as in rich ones, but there it appears under a different guise. Modernized poverty in poor nations affects more people more visibly but also – for the moment – more superficially. Two-thirds of all children in Latin America leave school before finishing the fifth grade, but these 'desertores' are not therefore as badly off as they would be in the United States.

Few countries today remain victims of classical poverty, which was stable and less disabling. Most countries in Latin America have reached the 'take-off' point towards economic development and competitive consumption, and thereby towards modernized poverty: their citizens have learned to think rich and live poor. Their laws make six to ten years of school obligatory. Not only in Argentina but also in Mexico or Brazil the average citizen defines an adequate education by North American standards, even though the chance of getting such prolonged schooling is limited to a tiny minority. In these countries the majority is already hooked on school, that is, they are schooled in a sense of inferiority towards the better schooled. Their fanaticism in favour of school makes it possible to exploit them doubly: it permits increasing allocation of public funds for the education of a few and increasing acceptance of social control by the many.

Paradoxically, the belief that universal schooling is absolutely necessary is most firmly held in those countries where the fewest people have been – and will be – served by schools. Yet in Latin America different paths towards education could still be taken by the majority of parents and children. Proportionately, national savings invested in schools and teachers might be higher than in rich countries, but these investments are totally insufficient to serve the majority by making even four years of school attendance possible. Fidel Castro talks as if he wanted to go in the direction of deschooling when he promises that by 1980 Cuba will be able to dissolve its university since all of life in Cuba will be an educational experience. At the grammar-school and high-school level, however, Cuba, like all other Latin American countries, acts as though passage through a period defined as the 'school age' were an unquestionable goal for all, delayed merely by a temporary shortage of resources.

The twin deceptions of increased treatment, as actually provided in the United States – and as merely promised in Latin America – complement each other. The Northern poor are being disabled by the same twelve-year treatment whose lack brands the Southern poor as hopelessly backward. Neither in North America nor in Latin America do the poor get equality from obligatory schools. But in both places the mere existence of school discourages and disables the poor from taking control of their own learning. All over the world the school has an anti-educational effect on society: school is recognized as the institution which specializes in education. The failures of school are taken by most people as a proof that education is a very costly, very complex, always arcane and frequently almost impossible task.

School appropriates the money, men and goodwill available for education and in addition discourages other institutions from assuming educational tasks. Work, leisure, politics, city living and even family life depend on schools for the habits and knowledge they presuppose, instead of becoming themselves the means of education. Simultaneously both schools and the other institutions which depend on them are priced out of the market.

In the United States the per capita costs of schooling have risen almost as fast as the cost of medical treatment. But increased treatment by both doctors and teachers has shown steadily declining results. Medical expenses concentrated on those above forty-five have doubled several times over a period of forty years with a resulting 3 per cent increase in life expectancy in men. The increase in educational expenditures has produced even stranger results; otherwise President Nixon could not have been moved in the spring of 1970 to promise that every child shall soon have the 'Right to Read' before leaving school.

In the United States it would take eighty thousand million dollars per year to provide what educators regard as equal treatment for all in grammar and high school. This is well over twice the thirty-six thousand million now being spent. Independent cost projections prepared at the Department of Health, Education and Welfare and the University of Florida indicate that by 1974 the comparable figures will be 107 thousand million dollars as against the forty-five thousand million now projected, and these figures wholly omit the enormous costs of what is called 'higher education', for which demand is growing even faster. The United States, which spent nearly eighty thousand million dollars in 1969 for 'defence' including its deployment in Vietnam, is obviously too poor to provide equal schooling. The President's committee for the study of school finance should ask not how to support or how to trim such increasing costs, but how they can be avoided.

Equal obligatory schooling must be recognized as at least economically unfeasible. In Latin America the amount of public money spent on each graduate student is between 350 and 1500 times the amount spent on the median citizen (that is, the citizen who holds the middle ground between the poorest and the richest). In the United States the discrepancy is smaller, but the discrimination is keener. The richest parents, some 10 per cent, can afford private education for their children and help them to benefit from foundation grants. But in addition they obtain ten times the per capita amount of public funds if this is compared with the per capita expenditure made on the children of the 10 per cent who are poorest. The principal reasons for this are that rich children stay longer in school, that a year in a university is disproportionalily more expensive than a year in high school, and that most private universities depend – at least indirectly – on tax-derived finances.

Obligatory schooling inevitably polarizes a society; it also grades the nations of the world according to an international caste system. Countries are rated like castes whose educational dignity is determined by the average years of schooling of its citizens, a rating which is closely related to per capita gross national product, and much more painful.

The paradox of the schools is evident: increased expenditure escalates their destructiveness at home and abroad. This paradox must be made a public issue. It is now generally accepted that the physical environment will soon be destroyed by biochemical pollution unless we reverse current trends in the production of physical goods. It should also be recognized that social and personal life is threatened equally by HEW pollution, the inevitable by-product of obligatory and competitive consumption of welfare.

The escalation of the schools is as destructive as the escalation of weapons but less visibly so. Everywhere in the world school costs have risen faster than enrolments and faster than the GNP; everywhere expenditures on school fall even further behind the expectations of parent, teacher and pupils. Everywhere this situation discourages both the motivation and the financing for large-scale planning for non-schooled learning. The United States is proving to the world that no country can be rich enough to afford a school system that meets the demands this same system creates simply by existing, because a successful school system schools parents and pupils to the supreme value of a larger school system, the cost of which increases disproportionately as higher grades are in demand and become scarce.

Rather than calling equal schooling temporarily unfeasible, we must recognize that it is, in principle, economically absurd, and that to attempt it is intellectually emasculating, socially polarizing and destructive of the credibility of the political system which promotes it. The ideology of obligatory schooling admits of no logical limits. The White House recently provided a good example. Dr Hutschnecker, the 'psychiatrist' who treated Mr Nixon before he was qualified as a candidate, recommended to the President that all children between six and eight be professionally examined to ferret out those who have destructive tendencies, and that obligatory treatment be provided for them. If necessary, their re-education in special institutions should be required. This memorandum from his doctor the President sent for evaluation to HEW. Indeed, preventive concentration camps for pre-delinquents would be a logical improvement over the school system.

Equal educational opportunity is, indeed, both a desirable and a feasible goal, but to equate this with obligatory schooling is to confuse salvation with the Church. School has become the world religion of a modernized proletariat, and makes futile promises of salvation to the poor of the technological age. The nation-state has adopted it, drafting all citizens into a graded curriculum leading to sequential diplomas not unlike the initiation rituals and hieratic promotions of former times. The modern state has assumed the duty of enforcing the judgement of its educators through well-meant truant officers and job requirements, much as did the Spanish kings who enforced the judgements of their theologians through the conquistadors and the Inquisition.

Two centuries ago the United States led the world in a movement to disestablish the monopoly of a single church. Now we need the constitutional disestablishment of the monopoly of the school, and thereby of a system which legally combines prejudice with discrimination. The first article of a bill of rights for a modern, humanist society would correspond to the First Amendment to the US Constitution: 'The State shall make no law with respect to the establishment of education.' There shall be no ritual obligatory for all.

To make this disestablishment effective, we need a law forbidding discrimination in hiring, voting or admission to centres of learning based on previous attendance at some curriculum. This guarantee would not exclude performance tests of competence for a function or role, but would remove the present absurd discrimination in favour of the person who learns a given skill with the largest expenditure of public funds or – what is equally likely – has been able to obtain a diploma which has no relation to any useful skill or job. Only by protecting the citizen from being disqualified by anything in his career in school can a constitutional disestablishment of school become psychologically effective.

Neither learning nor justice is promoted by schooling because educators insist on packaging instruction with certification. Learning and the assignment of social roles are melted into schooling. Yet to learn means to acquire a new skill or insight, while promotion depends on an opinion which others have formed. Learning frequently is the result of instruction, but selection for a role or category in the job market increasingly depends on mere length of attendance.

Instruction is the choice of circumstances which facilitate learning. Roles are assigned by setting a curriculum of conditions which the candidate must meet if he is to make the grade. School links instruction – but not learning – to these roles. This is neither reasonable nor liberating. It is not reasonable because it does not link relevant qualities or competences to roles, but rather the process by which such qualities are supposed to be acquired. It is not liberating or educational because school reserves instruction to those whose every step in learning fits previously approved measures of social control.

Curriculum has always been used to assign social rank. At times it could be pre-natal: karma ascribes you to a caste and lineage to the aristocracy. Curriculum could take the form of a ritual, of sequential sacred ordinations, or it could consist of a succession of feats in war or hunting, or further advancement could be made to depend on a series of previous princely favours. Universal schooling was meant to detach role assignment from personal life history: it was meant to give everybody an equal chance to any office. Even now many people wrongly believe that school ensures the dependence of public trust on relevant learning achievements. However, instead of equalizing chances, the school system has monopolized their distribution.

To detach competence from curriculum, inquiries into a man's learning history must be made taboo, like inquiries into his political affiliation, church attendance, lineage, sex habits or racial background. Laws forbidding discrimination on the basis of prior schooling must be enacted. Laws, of course, cannot stop prejudice against the unschooled – nor are they meant to force anyone to intermarry with an autodidact – but they can discourage unjustified discrimination.

A second major illusion on which the school system rests is that most learning is the result of teaching. Teaching, it is true, may contribute to certain kinds of learning under certain circumstances. But most people acquire most of their knowledge outside school, and in school only in so far as school, in a few rich countries, has become their place of confinement during an increasing part of their lives.

Most learning happens casually, and even most intentional learning is not the result of programmed instruction. Normal children learn their first language casually, although faster if their parents pay attention to them. Most people who learn a second language well do so as a result of odd circumstances and not of sequential teaching. They go to live with their grandparents, they travel, or they fall in love with a foreigner. Fluency in reading is also more often than not a result of such extracurricular activities. Most people who read widely, and with pleasure, merely believe that they learned to do so in school; when challenged, they easily discard this illusion.

But the fact that a great deal of learning even now seems to happen casually and as a by-product of some other activity defined as work or leisure does not mean that planned learning does not benefit from planned instruction and that both do not stand in need of improvement. The strongly motivated student who is faced with the task of acquiring a new and complex skill may benefit greatly from the discipline now associated with the old-fashioned schoolmaster who taught reading, Hebrew, catechism or multiplication by rote. School has now made this kind of drill teaching rare and disreputable, yet there are many skills which a motivated student with normal aptitude can master in a matter of a few months if taught in this traditional way. This is as true of codes as of their encipherment; of second and third languages as of reading and writing; and equally of special languages such as algebra, computer programming, chemical analysis, or of manual skills like typing, watchmaking, plumbing, wiring, TV repair; or for that matter dancing, driving and diving.

In certain cases acceptance into a learning programme aimed at a specific skill might presuppose competence in some other skill, but it should certainly not be made to depend upon the process by which such prerequisite skills were acquired. TV repair presupposes literacy and some maths; diving, good swimming; and driving, very little of either.

Progress in learning skills is measurable. The optimum resources in time and materials needed by an average motivated adult can be easily estimated. The cost of teaching a second Western European language to a high level of fluency ranges between four and six hundred dollars in the United States, and for an Oriental tongue the time needed for instruction might be doubled. This would still be very little compared with the cost of twelve years of schooling in New York City (a condition for acceptance of a worker into the Sanitation Department) – almost fifteen thousand dollars. No doubt not only the teacher but also the printer and the pharmacist protect their trades through the public illusion that training for them is very expensive.

At present schools pre-empt most educational funds. Drill instruction which costs less than comparable schooling is now a privilege of those rich enough to bypass the schools, and those whom either the army or big business sends through in-service training. In a programme of progressive deschooling of US education, at first the resources available for drill training would be limited. But ultimately there should be no obstacle for anyone at any time of his life to be able to choose instruction among hundreds of definable skills at public expense.

Right now educational credit good at any skill centre could be provided in limited amounts for people of all ages, and not just to the poor. I envisage such credit in the form of an educational passport or an 'edu-credit card' provided to each citizen at birth. In order to favour the poor, who probably would not use their yearly grants early in life, a provision could be made that interest accrued to later users of cumulated 'entitlements'. Such credits would permit most people to acquire the skills most in demand, at their convenience, better, faster, cheaper and with fewer undesirable side-effects than in school.

Potential skill teachers are never scarce for long because, on the one hand, demand for a skill grows only with its performance within a community and, on the other, a man exercising a skill could also teach it. But, at present, those using skills which are in demand and do require a human teacher are discouraged from sharing these skills with others. This is done either by teachers who monopolize the licences or by unions which protect their trade interests. Skill centres which would be judged by customers on their results, and not on the personnel they employ or the process they use, would open unsuspected working opportunities, frequently even for those who are now considered unemployable. Indeed, there is no reason why such skill centres should not be at the work place itself, with the employer and his work force supplying instruction as well as jobs to those who choose to use their educational credits in this way.

In 1956 there arose a need to teach Spanish quickly to several hundred teachers, social workers and ministers from the New York Archdiocese so that they could communicate with Puerto Ricans. My friend Gerry Morris announced over a Spanish radio station that he needed native speakers from Harlem. Next day some two hundred teenagers lined up in front of his office, and he selected four dozen of them – many of them school dropouts. He trained them in the use of the US Foreign Service Institute (FSI) Spanish manual, designed for use by linguists with graduate training, and within a week his teachers were on their own – each in charge of four New Yorkers who wanted to speak the language. Within six months the mission was accomplished. Cardinal Spellman could claim that he had 127 parishes in which at least three staff members could communicate in Spanish. No school programme could have matched these results.

Skill teachers are made scarce by the belief in the value of licences. Certification constitutes a form of market manipulation and is plausible only to a schooled mind. Most teachers of arts and trades are less skilful, less inventive and less communicative than the best craftsmen and tradesmen. Most high-school teachers of Spanish or French do not speak the language as correctly as their pupils might after half a year of competent drills. Experiments conducted by Angel Quintero in Puerto Rico suggest that many young teenagers, if given the proper incent-

ives, programmes and access to tools, are better than most schoolteachers at introducing their peers to the scientific exploration
of plants, stars and matter, and to the discovery of how and why
a motor or a radio functions.

Opportunities for skill-learning can be vastly multiplied if
we open the 'market'. This depends on matching the right
teacher with the right student when he is highly motivated in an
intelligent programme, without the constraint of curriculum.

Free and competing drill instruction is a subversive blasphemy
to the orthodox educator. It dissociates the acquisition of skills
from 'humane' education, which schools package together, and
thus it promotes unlicenced learning no less than unlicenced
teaching for unpredictable purposes.

There is currently a proposal on record which seems at first
to make a great deal of sense. It has been prepared by Christopher Jencks of the Center for the Study of Public Policy and is
sponsored by the Office of Economic Opportunity. It proposes
to put educational 'entitlements' or tuition grants into the
hands of parents and students for expenditure in the schools of
their choice. Such individual entitlements could indeed be an
important step in the right direction. We need a guarantee of
the right of each citizen to an equal share of tax-derived educational resources, the right to verify this share and the right to
sue for it if denied. It is one form of a guarantee against
regressive taxation.

The Jencks proposal, however, begins with the ominous statement that 'conservatives, liberals and radicals have all complained
at one time or another that the American educational system
gives professional educators too little incentive to provide
high-quality education to most children'. The proposal con-
demns itself by proposing tuition grants which would have to
be spent on schooling.

This is like giving a lame man a pair of crutches and stipulat-
ing that he uses them only if the ends are tied togther. As the
proposal for tuition grants now stands, it plays into the hands
not only of the professional educators but of racists, promoters
of religious schools and others whose interests are socially divisive. Above all, educational entitlements restricted to use within
schools play into the hands of all those who want to continue to

live in a society in which social advancement is tied not to proven knowledge but to the learning pedigree by which it is supposedly acquired. This discrimination in favour of schools which dominates Jencks's discussion on refinancing education could discredit one of the most critically needed principles for educational reform: the return of the initiative and accountability for learning to the learner or his most immediate tutor.

The deschooling of society implies a recognition of the two-faced nature of learning. An insistence on skill drill alone could be a disaster; equal emphasis must be placed on other kinds of learning. But if schools are the wrong places for learning a skill, they are even worse places for getting an education. School does both tasks badly, partly because it does not distinguish between them. School is inefficient in skill instruction especially because it is curricular. In most schools a programme which is meant to improve one skill is chained always to another irrelevant task. History is tied to advancement in maths, and class attendance to the right to use the playground.

Schools are even less efficient in the arrangement of the circumstances which encourage the open-ended, exploratory use of acquired skills, for which I will reserve the term 'liberal education'. The main reason for this is that school is obligatory and becomes schooling for schooling's sake: an enforced stay in the company of teachers, which pays off in the doubtful privilege of more such company. Just as skill instruction must be freed from curriculur restraints, so must liberal education be dissociated from obligatory attendance. Both skill-learning and education for inventive and creative behaviour can be aided by institutional arrangement, but they are of a different, frequently opposed nature.

Most skills can be acquired and improved by drills, because skill implies the mastery of definable and predictable behaviour. Skill instruction can rely, therefore, on the simulation of circumstances in which the skill will be used. Education in the exploratory and creative use of skills, however, cannot rely on drills. Education can be the outcome of instruction, though instruction of a kind fundamentally opposed to drill. It relies on the relationship between partners who already have some of the keys which give access to memories stored in and by the community. It relies on the critical intent of all those who use memories creatively. It relies on the surprise of the unexpected question which opens new doors for the inquirer and his partner.

The skill instructor relies on the arrangement of set circumstances which permit the learner to develop standard responses. The educational guide or master is concerned with helping matching partners to meet so that learning can take place. He matches individuals starting from their own, unresolved questions. At the most he helps the pupil to formulate his puzzlement since only a clear statement will give him the power to find his match, moved like him, at the moment, to explore the same issue in the same context.

Matching partners for educational purposes initially seems more difficult to imagine than finding skill instructors and partners for a game. One reason is the deep fear which school has implanted in us, a fear which makes us censorious. The unlicenced exchange of skills – even undesirable skills – is more predictable and therefore seems less dangerous than the unlimited opportunity for meeting among people who share an issue which for them, at the moment, is socially, intellectually and emotionally important.

The Brazilian teacher Paulo Freire knows this from experience. He discovered that any adult can begin to read in a matter of forty hours if the first words he deciphers are charged with political meaning. Freire trains his teachers to move into a village and to discover the words which designate current important issues, such as the access to a well or the compound interest on the debts owed to the *patron*. In the evening the villagers meet for the discussion of these key words. They begin to realize that each word stays on the blackboard even after its sound has faded. The letters continue to unlock reality and to make it manageable as a problem. I have frequently witnessed how discussants grow in social awareness and how they are impelled to take political action as fast as they learn to read. They seem to take reality into their hands as they write it down.

I remember the man who complained about the weight of pencils: they were difficult to handle because they did not weigh as much as a shovel; and I remember another who on his way to

work stopped with his companions and wrote the word they were discussing with his hoe on the ground: '*agua*'. Since 1962 my friend Freire has moved from exile to exile, mainly because he refuses to conduct his sessions around words which are pre-selected by approved educators, rather than those which his discussants bring to the class.

The educational matchmaking among people who have been successfully schooled is a different task. Those who do not need such assistance are a minority, even among the readers of serious journals. The majority cannot and should not be rallied for discussion around a slogan, a word or a picture. But the idea remains the same: they should be able to meet around a problem chosen and defined by their own initiative. Creative, exploratory learning requires peers currently puzzled about the same terms or problems. Large universities make the futile attempt to match them by multiplying their courses, and they generally fail since they are bound to curriculum, course structure and bureaucratic administration. In schools, including universities, most resources are spent to purchase the time and motivation of a limited number of people to take up predetermined problems in a ritually defined setting. The most radical alternative to school would be a network or service which gave each man the same opportunity to share his current concern with others motivated by the same concern.

Let me give, as an example of what I mean, a description of how an intellectual match might work in New York City. Each man, at any given moment and at a minimum price, could identify himself to a computer with his address and telephone number, indicating the book, article, film or recording on which he seeks a partner for discussion. Within days he could receive by mail the list of others who recently had taken the same initiative. This list would enable him by telephone to arrange for a meeting with persons who initially would be known exclusively by the fact that they requested a dialogue about the same subject.

Matching people according to their interest in a particular title is radically simple. It permits identification only on the basis of a mutual desire to discuss a statement recorded by a third person, and it leaves the initiative of arranging the meeting to the individual. Three objections are usually raised against this skeletal purity. I take them up not only to clarify the theory that I want to illustrate by my proposal – for they highlight the deep-seated resistance to deschooling education, to separating learning from social control – but also because they may help to suggest existing resources which are not now used for learning purposes.

The first objection is: Why cannot self-identification be based also on an *idea* or an issue? Certainly such subjective terms could also be used in a computer system. Political parties, churches, unions, clubs, neighbourhood centres and professional societies already organize their educational activities in this way and in effect they act as schools. They all match people in order to explore certain 'themes'; and these are dealt with in courses, seminars and curricula in which presumed 'common interests' are prepackaged. Such theme-matching is by definition teacher-centred: it requires an authoritarian presence to define for the participants the starting point for their discussion.

By contrast, matching by the title of a book, film, etc., in its pure form leaves it to the author to define the special language, the terms, and the framework within which a given problem or fact is stated; and it enables those who accept this starting point to identify themselves to one another. For instance, matching people around the idea of 'cultural revolution' usually leads either to confusion or to demagoguery. On the other hand, matching those interested in helping each other understand a specific article by Mao, Marcuse, Freud or Goodman stands in the great tradition of liberal learning from Plato's Dialogues, which are built around presumed statements by Socrates, to Aquinas's commentaries on Peter the Lombard. The idea of matching by title is thus radically different from the theory on which the 'Great Books' clubs, for example, were built: instead of relying on the selection by some Chicago professors, any two partners can choose any book for further analysis.

The second objection asks: Why not let the identification of match seekers include information on age, background, world view, competence, experience or other defining characteristics? Again, there is no reason why such discriminatory restrictions could not and should not be built into some of the many universities – with or without walls – which could use title-matching as their basic organizational device. I could conceive of a system designed to encourage meetings of interested persons at which the author of the book chosen would be present or represented; or a system which guaranteed the presence of a competent adviser; or one to which only students registered in a department or school had access; or one which permitted meetings only between people who defined their special approach to the title under discussion. Advantages for achieving specific goals of learning could be found for each of these restrictions. But I fear that, more often than not, the real reason for proposing such restrictions is contempt arising from the presumption that people are ignorant: educators want to avoid the ignorant meeting the ignorant around a text which they may not understand and which they read *only* because they are interested in it.

The third objection: Why not provide match seekers with incidental assistance that will facilitate their meetings – with space, schedules, screening and protection? This is now done by schools with all the inefficiency characterizing large bureaucracies. If we left the initiative for meetings to the match seekers themselves, organizations which nobody now classifies as educational would probably do the job much better. I think of restaurant owners, publishers, telephone-answering services, department-store managers, and even commuter-train executives who could promote their services by rendering them attractive for educational meetings.

At a first meeting in a coffee shop, say, the partners might establish their identities by placing the book under discussion next to their cups. People who took the initiative to arrange for such meetings would soon learn what items to quote to meet the people they sought. The risk that the self-chosen discussion with one or several strangers might lead to a loss of time, disappointment or even unpleasantness is certainly smaller than the same risk taken by a college applicant. A computer-arranged meeting to discuss an article in a national magazine, held in a coffee shop off Fourth Avenue, would obligate none of the participants to stay in the company of his new acquaintances for longer than it took to drink a cup of coffee, nor would he have to meet any of them ever again. The chance that it would help to pierce the opaqueness of life in a modern city and further new friendship, self-chosen work and critical reading is high. (The fact that a record of personal readings and meetings could be obtained thus by the FBI is undeniable; that this should still worry anybody in 1970 is only amusing to a free man, who willy-nilly contributes his share in order to drown snoopers in the irrelevancies they gather.)

Both the exchange of skills and matching of partners are based on the assumption that education for all means education by all. Not the draft into a specialized institution but only the mobilization of the whole population can lead to popular culture. The equal right of each man to exercise his competence to learn and to instruct is now pre-empted by certified teachers. The teachers' competence, in turn, is restricted to what may be done in school. And, further, work and leisure are alienated from each other as a result: the spectator and the worker alike are supposed to arrive at the work place all ready to fit into a routine prepared for them. Adaptation in the form of a product's design, instruction and publicity shapes them for their role as much as formal education by schooling. A radical alternative to a schooled society requires not only new formal mechanisms for the formal acquisition of skills and their educational use. A deschooled society implies a new approach to incidental or informal education.

Incidental education cannot any longer return to the forms which learning took in the village or the medieval town. Traditional society was more like a set of concentric circles of meaningful structures, while modern man must learn how to find meaning in many structures to which he is only marginally related. In the village, language and architecture and work and religion and family customs were consistent with one another, mutually explanatory and reinforcing. To grow into one implied a growth into the others. Even specialized apprenticeship was a by-product of specialized activities, such as shoemaking or the singing of psalms. If an apprentice never became a master or a scholar, he still contributed to making shoes or to making church services solemn. Education did not compete for time with either work or leisure. Almost all education was complex, lifelong and unplanned.

Contemporary society is the result of conscious designs, and

educational opportunities must be designed into them. Our reliance on specialized, full-time instruction through school will
now decrease, and we must find more ways to learn and teach:
the educational quality of all institutions must increase again.
But this is a very ambiguous forecast. It could mean that men
in the modern city will be increasingly the victims of an effective process of total instruction and manipulation once they are
deprived of even the tenuous pretence of critical independence
which liberal schools now provide for at least some of their
pupils.

It could also mean that men will shield themselves less behind
certificates acquired in school and thus gain in courage to 'talk
back' and thereby control and instruct the institutions in which
they participate. To ensure the latter we must learn to estimate
the social value of work and leisure by the educational give-and-
take for which they offer opportunity. Effective participation in
the politics of a street, a work place, the library, a news programme or a hospital is therefore the best measuring stick to evaluate
their level as educational institutions.

I recently spoke to a group of junior-high-school students in
the process of organizing a resistance movement to their obligatory draft into the next class. Their slogan was 'participation
– not simulation'. They were disappointed that this was understood as a demand for less rather than for more education, and
reminded me of the resistance which Karl Marx put up against
a passage in the Gotha programme, which – one hundred years
ago – wanted to outlaw child labour. He opposed the proposal
in the interest of the education of the young, which could happen only at work. If the greatest fruit of man's labour should be
the education he receives from it and the opportunity which
work gives him to initiate the education of others, then the
alienation of modern society in a pedagogical sense is even worse
than its economic alienation.

The major obstacle on the way to a society that truly educates
was well defined by a black friend of mine in Chicago, who told
me that our imagination was 'all schooled up'. We permit the
state to ascertain the universal educational deficiencies of its
citizens and establish one specialized agency to treat them. We
thus share in the delusion that we can distinguish between what

is necessary education for others and what is not, just as former generations established laws which defined what was sacred and what was profane.

Durkheim recognized that this ability to divide social reality into two realms was the very essence of formal religion. There are, he reasoned, religions without the supernatural and religions without gods, but none which does not subdivide the world into things and times and persons that are sacred and others that as a consequence are profane. Durkheim's insight can be applied to the sociology of education, for school is radically divisive in a similar way.

The very existence of obligatory schools divides any society. into two realms: some time spans and processes and treatments and professions are 'academic' or 'pedagogic', and others are not. The power of school thus to divide social reality has no boundaries: education becomes unwordly and the world becomes non-educational.

Since Bonhoeffer contemporary theologians have pointed to the confusions now reigning between the Biblical message and institutionalized religion. They point to the experience that Christian freedom and faith usually gain from secularization. Inevitably their statements sound blasphemous to many churchmen. Unquestionably, the educational process will gain from the deschooling of society even though this demand sounds to many schoolmen like treason to the enlightenment. But it is enlightenment itself that is now being snuffed out in the schools.

The secularization of the Christian faith depends on the dedication to it on the part of Christians rooted in the Church. In much the same way, the deschooling of education depends on the leadership of those brought up in the schools. Their curriculum cannot serve them as an alibi for the task: each of us remains responsible for what has been made of him, even though he may be able to do no more than accept this responsibility and serve as a warning to others.

2 Phenomenology of School

Some words become so flexible that they cease to be useful. 'School' and 'teaching' are such terms. Like an amoeba they fit into almost any interstice of the language. ABM will teach the Russians, IBM will teach Negro children, and the army can become the school of a nation.

The search for alternatives in education must therefore start with an agreement on what it is we mean by 'school'. This might be done in several ways. We could begin by listing the latent functions performed by modern school systems, such as custodial care, selection, indoctrination and learning. We could make a client analysis and verify which of these latent functions render a service or a disservice to teachers, employers, children, parents or the professions. We could survey the history of Western culture and the information gathered by anthropology in order to find institutions which played a role like that now performed by schooling. We could, finally, recall the many normative statements which have been made since the time of Comenius, or even since Quintilian, and discover which of these the modern school system most closely approaches. But any of these approaches would oblige us to start with certain assumptions about a relationship between school and education. To develop a language in which we can speak about school without such constant recourse to education, I have chosen to begin with something that might be called a phenomenology of public school. For this purpose I shall define 'school' as the age-specific, teacher-related process requiring full-time attendance at an obligatory curriculum.

Age

School groups people according to age. This grouping rests on three unquestioned premises. Children belong in school. Children

learn in school. Children can be taught only in school. I think
these unexamined premises deserve serious questioning.

We have grown accustomed to children. We have decided
that they should go to school, do as they are told, and have neither income nor families of their own. We expect them to know
their place and behave like children. We remember, whether nos-
talgically or bitterly, a time when we were children, too. We are
expected to tolerate the childish behaviour of children. Mankind, for us, is a species both afflicted and blessed with the task
of caring for children. We forget, however, that our present
concept of 'childhood' developed only recently in Western
Europe and more recently still in the Americas.*

Childhood as distinct from infancy, adolescence or youth was
unknown to most historical periods. Some Christian centuries
did not even have an eye for its bodily proportions. Artists de-
picted the infant as a miniature adult seated on his mother's
arm. Children appeared in Europe along with the pocket watch
and the Christian moneylenders of the Renaissance. Before our
century neither the poor nor the rich knew of children's dress,
children's games or the child's immunity from the law. Childhood belonged to the bourgeoisie. The worker's child, the peasant's child and the nobleman's child all dressed the way their
fathers dressed, played the way their fathers played and were
hanged by the neck as were their fathers. After the discovery of
'childhood' by the bourgeoisie all this changed. Only some
churches continued to respect for some time the dignity and
maturity of the young. Until the Second Vatican Council, each
child was instructed that a Christian reaches moral discernment
and freedom at the age of seven, and from then on is capable
of committing sins for which he may be punished by an eternity
in Hell. Towards the middle of this century, middle-class parents began to try and spare their children the impact of this doc-
trine, and their thinking about children now prevails in the practice of the Church.

Until the last century, 'children' of middle-class parents were
made at home with the help of preceptors and private schools.

*For parallel histories of modern capitalism and modern childhood
see Philippe Ariès, *Centuries of Childhood*, Knopf, 1962: Penguin,
1973.

Only with the advent of industrial society did the mass production of 'childhood' become feasible and come within the reach of the masses. The school system is a modern phenomenon, as is the childhood it produces.

Since most people today live outside industrial cities, most people today do not experience childhood. In the Andes you till the soil once you have become 'useful'. Before that, you watch the sheep. If you are well nourished, you should be useful by eleven, and otherwise by twelve. Recently, I was talking to my night watchman, Marcos, about his eleven-year-old son who works in a barbershop. I noted in Spanish that his son was still a 'niño'. Marcos, surprised, answered with a guileless smile: 'Don Ivan, I guess you're right.' Realizing that until my remark the father had thought of Marcos primarily as his 'son', I felt guilty for having drawn the curtain of childhood between two sensible persons. Of course if I were to tell the New York slum-dweller that his working son is still a 'child', he would show no surprise. He knows quite well that his eleven-year-old son should be allowed childhood, and resents the fact that he is not. The son of Marcos has yet to be afflicted with the yearning for childhood; the New Yorker's son feels deprived.

Most people around the world, then, either do not want or cannot get modern childhood for their offspring. But it also seems that childhood is a burden to a good number of those few who are allowed it. Many of them are simply forced to go through it and are not at all happy playing the child's role. Growing up through childhood means being condemned to a process of inhuman conflict between self-awareness and the role imposed by a society going through its own school age. Neither Stephen Daedalus nor Alexander Portnoy enjoyed childhood, and neither, I suspect, did many of us like to be treated as children.

If there were no age-specific and obligatory learning institution, 'childhood' would go out of production. The youth of rich nations would be liberated from its destructiveness, and poor nations would cease attempting to rival the childishness of the rich. If society were to outgrow its age of childhood, it would have to become livable for the young. The present disjunction between an adult society which pretends to be humane and a school environment which mocks reality could no longer be maintained.

The disestablishment of schools could also end the present discrimination against infants, adults and the old in favour of children throughout their adolescence and youth. The social decision to allocate educational resources preferably to those citizens who have outgrown the extraordinary learning capacity of their first four years and have not arrived at the height of their self-motivated learning will, in retrospect, probably appear as bizarre.

Institutional wisdom tells us that children need school. Institutional wisdom tells us that children learn in school. But this institutional wisdom is itself the product of schools because sound common sense tells us that only children can be taught in school. Only by segregating human beings in the category of childhood could we ever get them to submit to the authority of a schoolteacher.

Teachers and pupils

By definition, children are pupils. The demand for the milieu of childhood creates an unlimited market for accredited teachers. School is an institution built on the axiom that learning is the result of teaching. And institutional wisdom continues to accept this axiom, despite overwhelming evidence to the contrary.

We have all learned most of what we know outside school. Pupils do most of their learning without, and often despite, their teachers. Most tragically, the majority of men are taught their lesson by schools, even though they never go *to* school.

Everyone learns how to live outside school. We learn to speak, to think, to love, to feel, to play, to curse, to politick and to work without interference from a teacher. Even children who are under a teacher's care day and night are no exception to the rule. Orphans, idiots and schoolteachers' sons learn most of what they learn outside the 'educational' process planned for them. Teachers have made a poor showing in their attempt at increasing learning among the poor. Poor parents who want their children to go to school are less concerned about what they will learn than about the certificate and money they will earn. And middle-class parents commit their children to a teacher's care to keep them from learning what the poor learn on the streets. Increasingly, educational research demonstrates that children learn most of what teachers pretend to teach them from peer groups, from comics, from chance observations, and above all from mere participation in the ritual of school. Teachers, more often than not, obstruct such learning of subject matters as goes on in school.

Half of the people in our world never set foot in school. They have no contact with teachers, and they are deprived of the privilege of becoming dropouts. Yet they learn quite effectively the message which school teaches: that they should have school, and more and more of it. School instructs them in their own inferiority through the tax collector who makes them pay for it, or through the demagogue who raises their expectations of it, or through their children once the latter are hooked on it. So the poor are robbed of their self-respect by subscribing to a creed that grants salvation only through the school. At least the Church gave them a chance to repent at the hour of death. School leaves them with the expectation (a counterfeit hope) that their grandchildren will make it. That expectation is of course still more learning which comes from school but not from teachers.

Pupils have never credited teachers for most of their learning. Bright and dull alike have always relied on rote, reading and wit to pass their exams, motivated by the stick or by the carrot of a desired career.

Adults tend to romanticize their schooling. In retrospect, they attribute their learning to the teacher whose patience they learned to admire. But the same adults would worry about the mental health of a child who rushed home to tell them what he learned from his every teacher.

Schools create jobs for schoolteachers, no matter what their pupils learn from them.

Full-time attendance

Every month I see another list of proposals made by some US industry to AID, suggesting the replacement of Latin American 'classroom practitioners' either by disciplined systems administrators or just by TV. In the United States teaching as a team enterprise of educational researchers, designers and technicians is gaining acceptance. But, no matter whether the teacher is a schoolmarm or a team of men in white coats, and no matter whether they succeed in teaching the subject matter listed in the catalogue or whether they fail, the professional teacher creates a sacred milieu.

Uncertainty about the future of professional teaching puts the classroom into jeopardy. Were educational professionals to specialize in promoting learning, they would have to abandon a system which calls for between 750 and 1000 gatherings a year. But of course teachers do a lot more. The institutional wisdom of schools tells parents, pupils and educators that the teacher, if he is to teach, must exercise his authority in a sacred precinct. This is true even for teachers whose pupils spend most of their school time in a classroom without walls.

School, by its very nature, tends to make a total claim on the time and energies of its participants. This, in turn, makes the teacher into custodian, preacher and therapist.

In each of these three roles the teacher bases his authority on a different claim. The *teacher-as-custodian* acts as a master of ceremonies, who guides his pupils through a drawn-out labyrinthine ritual. He arbitrates the observance of rules and administers the intricate rubrics of initiation to life. At his best, he sets the stage for the acquisition of some skill as schoolmasters always have. Without illusions of producing any profound learning, he drills his pupils in some basic routines.

The *teacher-as-moralist* substitutes for parents, God or the state. He indoctrinates the pupil about what is right or wrong, not only in school but also in society at large. He stands *in loco parentis* for each one and thus ensures that all feel themselves children of the same state.

The *teacher-as-therapist* feels authorized to delve into the personal life of his pupil in order to help him grow as a person. When this function is exercised by a custodian and preacher, it usually means that he persuades the pupil to submit to a domestication of his vision of truth and his sense of what is right.

The claim that a liberal society can be founded on the modern school is paradoxical. The safeguards of individual freedom are all cancelled in the dealings of a teacher with his pupil. When the schoolteacher fuses in his person the functions of judge, ideologue, and doctor, the fundamental style of society is perverted by the very process which should prepare life. A teacher who combines these three powers contributes to the warping of the child much more than the laws which establish his legal or economic minority, or restrict his right to free assembly or abode.

Teachers are by no means the only professionals who offer therapy. Psychiatrists, guidance counsellors and job counsellors, even lawyers, help their clients to decide, to develop their personalities and to learn. Yet common sense tells the client that such professionals should abstain from imposing their opinion of what is right or wrong, or from forcing anyone to follow their advice. Schoolteachers and ministers are the only professionals who feel entitled to pry into the private affairs of their clients at the same time as they preach to a captive audience.

Children are protected by neither the First nor the Fifth Amendment when they stand before that secular priest, the teacher. The child must confront a man who wears an invisible triple crown, like the papal tiara, the symbol of triple authority combined in one person. For the child, the teacher pontificates as pastor, prophet and priest – he is at once guide, teacher and administrator of a sacred ritual. He combines the claims of medieval popes in a society constituted under the guarantee that these claims shall never be exercised together by one established and obligatory institution – church or state.

Defining children as full-time pupils permits the teacher to exercise a kind of power over their persons which is much less limited by constitutional and consuetudinal restrictions than the power wielded by the guardians of other social enclaves. Their chronological age disqualifies children from safeguards which are routine for adults in a modern asylum – madhouse, monastery or jail.

Under the authoritative eye of the teacher, several orders of value collapse into one. The distinctions between morality, legality and personal worth are blurred and eventually eliminated. Each transgression is made to be felt as a multiple offence. The offender is expected to feel that he has broken a rule, that he has behaved immorally, and that he has let himself down. A pupil who adroitly obtains assistance on an exam is told that he is an outlaw, morally corrupt and personally worthless.

Classroom attendance removes children from the everyday world of Western culture and plunges them into an environment far more primitive, magical and deadly serious. School could not create such an enclave within which the rules of ordinary reality are suspended, unless it physically incarcerated the young during many successive years on sacred territory. The attendance rule makes it possible for the schoolroom to serve as a magic womb, from which the child is delivered periodically at the schoolday's and school year's completion until he is finally expelled into adult life. Neither universal extended childhood nor the smothering atmosphere of the classroom could exist without schools. Yet schools, as compulsory channels for learning, could exist without either and be more repressive and destructive than anything we have come to know. To understand what it means to deschool society, and not just to reform the educational establishment, we must now focus on the hidden curriculum of schooling. We are not concerned here, directly, with the hidden curriculum of the ghetto streets which brands the poor or with the hidden curriculum of the drawing room which benefits the rich. We are rather concerned to call attention to the fact that the ceremonial or ritual of schooling itself constitutes such a hidden curriculum. Even the best of teachers cannot entirely protect his pupils from it. Inevitably, this hidden curriculum of schooling adds prejudice and guilt to the discrimination which a society practises against some of its members and compounds the privilege of others with a new title to condescend to the majority. Just as inevitably, this hidden curriculum serves as a ritual of initiation into a growth-oriented consumer society for rich and poor alike.

3 Ritualization of Progress

The university graduate has been schooled for selective service among the rich of the world. Whatever his or her claims of solidarity with the Third World, each American college graduate has had an education costing an amount five times greater than the median life income of half of humanity. A Latin American student is introduced to this exclusive fraternity by having at least 350 times as much public money spent on his education as on that of his fellow citizens of median income. With very rare exceptions, the university graduate from a poor country feels more comfortable with his North American and European colleagues than with his non-schooled compatriots, and all students are academically processed to be happy only in the company of fellow consumers of the products of the educational machine.

The modern university confers the privilege of dissent on those who have been tested and classified as potential money-makers or power-holders. No one is given tax funds for the leisure in which to educate himself or the right to educate others unless at the same time he can also be certified for achievement. Schools select for each successive level those who have, at earlier stages in the game, proved themselves good risks for the established order. Having a monopoly on both the resources for learning and the investiture of social roles, the university coopts the discoverer and the potential dissenter. A degree always leaves its indelible price tag on the curriculum of its consumer. Certified college graduates fit only into a world which puts a price tag on their heads, thereby giving them the power to define the level of expectations in their society. In each country the amount of consumption by the college graduate sets the standard for all others; if they would be civilized people on or off the job, they will aspire to the style of life of college graduates.

The university thus has the effect of imposing consumer

standards at work and at home, and it does so in every part of the world and under every political system. The fewer university graduates there are in a country, the more their cultivated demands are taken as models by the rest of the population. The gap between the consumption of the university graduate and that of the average citizen is even wider in Russia, China and Algeria than in the United States. Cars, aeroplane trips and tape recorders confer more visible distinction in a socialist country, where only a degree, and not just money, can procure them.

The ability of the university to fix consumer goals is something new. In many countries the university acquired this power only in the 1960s, as the delusion of equal access to public education began to spread. Before that the university protected an individual's freedom of speech, but did not automatically convert his knowledge into wealth. To be a scholar in the Middle Ages meant to be poor, even a beggar. By virtue of his calling, the medieval scholar learned Latin, became an outsider worthy of the scorn as well as the esteem of peasant and prince, burgher and cleric. To get ahead in the world, the scholastic first had to enter it by joining the civil service, preferably that of the Church. The old university was a liberated zone for discovery and the discussion of ideas both new and old. Masters and students gathered to read the texts of other masters, now long dead, and the living words of the dead masters gave new perspective to the fallacies of the present day. The university was then a community of acadmic quest and endemic unrest.

In the modern multiversity this community has fled to the fringes, where it meets in a pad, a professor's office or the chaplain's quarters. The structural purpose of the modern university has little to do with the traditional quest. Since Gutenburg, the exchange of disciplined, critical inquiry has, for the most part, moved from the 'chair' into print. The modern university has forfeited its chance to provide a simple setting for encounters which are both autonomous and anarchic, focused yet unplanned and ebullient, and has chosen instead to manage the process by which so-called research and instruction are produced.

The American university, since Sputnik, has been trying to catch up with the body count of Soviet graduates. Now the Germans are abandoning their academic tradition and are building 'campuses' in order to catch up with the Americans. During the present decade they want to increase their expenditure for grammar and high schools from fourteen to fifty-nine thousand million DM, and more than triple expenditures for higher learning. The French propose by 1980 to raise to 10 per cent of the GNP the amount spent on schools, and the Ford Foundation has been pushing poor countries in Latin America to raise per capita expenses for 'respectable' graduates towards North American levels. Students see their studies as the investment with the highest monetary return, and nations see them as a key factor in development.

For the majority who primarily seek a college degree, the university has lost no prestige, but since 1968 it has visibly lost standing among its believers. Students refuse to prepare for war, pollution and the perpetuation of prejudice. Teachers assist them in their challenge to the legitimacy of the government, its foreign policy, education and the American way of life. More than a few reject degrees and prepare for a life in a counter-culture, outside the certified society. They seem to choose the way of medieval Fraticelli and Alumbrados of the Reformation, the hippies and dropouts of their day. Others recognize the monopoly of the schools over the resources which they need to build a counter-society. They seek support from each other to live with integrity while submitting to the academic ritual. They form, so to speak, hotbeds of heresy right within the hierarchy.

Large parts of the general population, however, regard the modern mystic and the modern heresiarch with alarm. They threaten the consumer economy, democratic privilege and the self-image of America. But they cannot be wished away. Fewer and fewer can be reconverted by patience or coopted by subtlety – for instance, by appointing them to teach their heresy. Hence the search for means which would make it possible either to get rid of dissident individuals or to reduce the importance of the university which serves them as a base for protest.

The students and faculty who question the legitimacy of the university, and do so at high personal cost, certainly do not feel that they are setting consumer standards or abetting a production system. Those who have founded such groups as the Committee of Concerned Asian Scholars and the North American Congress on Latin America (NACLA) have been among the most effective in changing radically the perceptions of the realities of foreign countries for millions of young people. Still others have tried to formulate Marxian interpretations of American society or have been among those responsible for the flowering of communes. Their achievements add new strength to the argument that the existence of the university is necessary to guarantee continued social criticism.

There is no question that at present the university offers a unique combination of circumstances which allows some of its members to criticize the whole of society. It provides time, mobility, access to peers and information and a certain impunity – privileges not equally available to other segments of the population. But the university provides this freedom only to those who have already been deeply initiated into the consumer society and into the need for some kind of obligatory public schooling.

The school system today performs the threefold function common to powerful churches throughout history. It is simultaneously the repository of society's myth, the institutionalization of that myth's contradictions, and the locus of the ritual which reproduces and veils the disparities between myth and reality. Today the school system, and especially the university, provides ample opportunity for criticism of the myth and for rebellion against its institutional perversions. But the ritual which demands tolerance of the fundamental contradictions between myth and institution still goes largely unchallenged, for neither ideological criticism nor social action can bring about a new society. Only disenchantment with and detachment from the central social ritual and reform of that ritual can bring about radical change.

The American university has become the final stage of the most all-encompassing initiation rite the world has ever known. No society in history has been able to survive without ritual or myth, but ours is the first which has needed such a dull, protracted, destructive and expensive initiation into its myth. The contemporary world civilization is also the first one which has found it necessary to rationalize its fundamental initiation ritual in the name of education. We cannot begin a reform of education unless we first understand that neither individual learning nor social equality can be enhanced by the ritual of schooling. We cannot go beyond the consumer society unless we first understand that obligatory public schools inevitably reproduce such a society, no matter what is taught in them.

The project of demythologizing which I propose cannot be limited to the university alone. Any attempt to reform the university without attending to the system of which it is an integral part is like trying to do urban renewal in New York City from the twelfth storey up. Most current college-level reform looks like the building of high-rise slums. Only a generation which grows up without obligatory schools will be able to recreate the university.

The myth of institutionalized values

School initiates, too, the Myth of Unending Consumption. This modern myth is grounded in the belief that process inevitably produces something of value and, therefore, production necessarily produces demand. School teaches us that instruction produces learning. The existence of schools produces the demand for schooling. Once we have learned to need school, all our activities tend to take the shape of client relationships to other specialized institutions. Once the self-taught man or woman has been discredited, all non-professional activity is rendered suspect. In school we are taught that valuable learning is the result of attendance; that the value of learning increases with the amount of input; and, finally, that this value can be measured and documented by grades and certificates.

In fact, learning is the human activity which least needs manipulation by others. Most learning is not the result of instruction. It is rather the result of unhampered participation in a meaningful setting. Most people learn best by being 'with it', yet school makes them identify their personal cognitive growth with elaborate planning and manipulation.

Once a man or woman has accepted the need for school, he or she is easy prey for other institutions. Once young people have allowed their imaginations to be formed by curricular instruction, they are conditioned to institutional planning of every sort. 'Instruction' smothers the horizon of their imaginations. They cannot be betrayed, but only short-changed, because they have been taught to substitute expectations for hope. They will no longer be surprised, for good or ill, by other people, because they have been taught what to expect from every other person who has been taught as they were. This is true in the case of another person or in the case of a machine.

This transfer of responsibility from self to institution guarantees social regression, especially once it had been accepted as an obligation. So rebels against Alma Mater often 'make it' into her faculty instead of growing into the courage to infect others with their personal teaching and to assume responsibility for the results. This suggests the possibility of a new Oedipus story – Oedipus the Teacher, who 'makes' his mother in order to engender children with her. The man addicted to being taught seeks his security in compulsive teaching. The woman who experiences her knowledge as the result of a process wants to reproduce it in others.

The myth of measurement of values

The institutionalized values school instils are quantified ones. School initiates young people into a world where everything can be measured, including their imaginations, and, indeed, man himself.

But personal growth is not a measurable entity. It is growth in disciplined dissidence, which cannot be measured against any rod, or any curriculum, nor compared to someone else's achievement. In such learning one can emulate others only in imaginative endeavour, and follow in their footsteps rather than mimic their gait. The learning I prize is immeasurable re-creation.

School pretends to break learning up into subject 'matters', to build into the pupil a curriculum made of these prefabricated blocks, and to gauge the result on an international scale. People who submit to the standard of others for the measure of their own personal growth soon apply the same ruler to themselves. They no longer have to be put in their place, but put themselves into their assigned slots, squeeze themselves into the niche which they have been taught to seek, and, in the very process, put their fellows into their places, too, until everybody and everything fits.

People who have been schooled down to size let unmeasured experience slip out of their hands. To them, what cannot be measured becomes secondary, threatening. They do not have to be robbed of their creativity. Under instruction, they have unlearned to 'do' their thing or 'be' themselves, and value only what has been made or could be made.

Once people have the idea schooled into them that values can be produced and measured, they tend to accept all kinds of rankings. There is a scale for the development of nations, another for the intelligence of babies, and even progress towards peace can be calculated according to body count. In a schooled world the road to happiness is paved with a consumer's index.

The myth of packaging values

School sells curriculum – a bundle of goods made according to the same process and having the same structure as other merchandise. Curriculum production for most schools begins with allegedly scientific research, on whose basis educational engineers predict future demand and tools for the assembly line, within the limits set by budgets and taboos. The distributor-teacher delivers the finished product to the consumer-pupil, whose reactions are carefully studied and charted to provide research data for the preparation of the next model, which may be 'ungraded', 'student-designed', 'team-taught', 'visually-aided' or 'issue-centred'.

The result of the curriculum production process looks like any other modern staple. It is a bundle of planned meanings, a package of values, a commodity whose 'balanced appeal' makes it marketable to a sufficiently large number to justify the cost of production. Consumer-pupils are taught to make their desires conform to marketable values. Thus they are made to feel guilty if they do not behave according to the predictions of consumer research by getting the grades and certificates that will place them in the job category they have been led to expect.

Educators can justify more expensive curricula on the basis of their observation that learning difficulties rise proportionately with the cost of the curriculum. This is an application of Parkinson's Law that work expands with the resources available to do it. This law can be verified on all levels of school: for instance, reading difficulties have been a major issue in French schools only since their per capita expenditures have approached US levels of 1950 – when reading difficulties became a major issue in US schools.

In fact, healthy students often redouble their resistance to teaching as they find themselves more comprehensively manipulated. This resistance is due not to the authoritarian style of a public school or the seductive style of some free schools, but to the fundamental approach common to all schools – the idea that one person's judgement should determine what and when another person must learn.

The myth of self-perpetuating progress

Even when accompanied by declining returns in learning, paradoxically, rising per capita instructional costs increase the value of the pupil in his or her own eyes and on the market. At almost any cost, school pushes the pupil up to the level of competitive curricular consumption, into progress to ever higher levels. Expenditures to motivate the student to stay on in school skyrocket as he climbs the pyramid. On higher levels they are disguised as new football stadiums, chapels or programmes called International Education. If it teaches nothing else, school teaches the value of escalation: the value of the American way of doing things.

The Vietnam war fits the logic of the moment. Its success has been measured by the numbers of persons effectively treated by cheap bullets delivered at immense cost, and this brutal calculus is unashamedly called 'body count'. Just as business is business, the never-ending accumulation of money, so war is killing, the never-ending accumulation of dead bodies. In like manner, education is schooling, and this open-ended process is counted in pupil-hours. The various processes are irreversible and self-justifying. By economic standards the country gets richer and richer. By death-accounting standards the nation goes on winning its war forever. And by school standards the population becomes increasingly educated.

School programmes hunger for progressive intake of instruction, but even if the hunger leads to steady absorption, it never yields the joy of knowing something to one's satisfaction. Each subject comes packaged with the instruction to go on consuming one 'offering' after another, and last year's wrapping is always

obsolete for this year's consumer. The textbook racket builds on
this demand. Educational reformers promise each new generation the latest and the best, and the public is schooled into
demanding what they offer. Both the dropout who is forever
reminded of what he missed and the graduate who is made to feel
inferior to the new breed of student know exactly where they
stand in the ritual of rising deceptions and continue to support
a society which euphemistically calls the widening frustration
gap a 'revolution of rising expectations'.

But growth conceived as open-ended consumption – eternal
progress – can never lead to maturity. Commitment to unlimited
quantitative increase vitiates the possibility of organic development.

Ritual game and the new world religion

The school-leaving age in developed nations outpaces the rise
in life expectancy. The two curves will intersect in a decade and
create a problem for Jessica Mitford and professionals concerned with 'terminal education'. I am reminded of the late
Middle Ages, when the demand for Church services outgrew a
lifetime, and 'Purgatory' was created to purify souls under the
pope's control before they could enter eternal peace. Logically,
this led first to a trade in indulgences and then to an attempt at
Reformation. The Myth of Unending Consumption now takes
the place of belief in life everlasting.

Arnold Toynbee has pointed out that the decadence of a great
culture is usually accompanied by the rise of a new World
Church which extends hope to the domestic proletariat while
serving the needs of a new warrior class. School seems eminently
suited to be the World Church of our decaying culture. No institution could better veil from its participants the deep discrepancy between social principles and social reality in today's world.
Secular, scientific and death-denying, it is of a piece with the
modern mood. Its classical, critical veneer makes it appear plu-
ralist if not anti-religious. Its curriculum both defines science
and is itself defined by so-called scientific research. No one com-
pletes school – yet. It never closes its doors on anyone without
first offering him one more chance: at remedial, adult and continuing education.

School serves as an effective creator and sustainer of social myth because of its structure as a ritual game of graded promotions. Introduction into this gambling ritual is much more important than what or how something is taught. It is the game itself that schools, that gets into the blood and becomes a habit. A whole society is initiated into the Myth of Unending Consumption of services. This happens to the degree that token participation in the open-ended ritual is made compulsory and compulsive everywhere. School directs ritual rivalry into an international game which obliges competitors to blame the world's ills on those who cannot or will not play. School is a ritual of initiation which introduces the neophyte to the sacred race of progressive consumption, a ritual of propitiation whose academic priests mediate between the faithful and the gods of privilege and power, a ritual of expiation which sacrifices its dropouts, branding them as scapegoats of underdevelopment.

Even those who spend at best a few years in school – and this is the overwhelming majority in Latin America, Asia and Africa – learn to feel guilty because of their underconsumption of schooling. In Mexico six grades of school are legally obligatory. Children born into the lower economic third have only two chances in three to make it into the first grade. If they make it, they have four chances in one hundred to finish obligatory schooling by the sixth grade. If they are born into the middle third group, their chances increase to twelve out of a hundred. With these rules, Mexico is more successful than most of the other twenty-five Latin American republics in providing public education.

Everywhere, all children know that they were given a chance, albeit an unequal one, in an obligatory lottery, and the presumed equality of the international standard now compounds their original poverty with the self-inflicted discrimination accepted by the dropout. They have been schooled to the belief in rising expectations and can now rationalize their growing frustration outside school by accepting their rejection from scholastic grace. They are excluded from Heaven because, once baptized, they did not go to church. Born in original sin, they are baptized into first grade, but go to Gehenna (which in Hebrew means 'slum') because of their personal faults. As Max Weber traced the social

effects of the belief that salvation belonged to those who ac-
cumulated wealth, we can now observe that grace is reserved for
those who accumulate years in school.

The coming kingdom: the universalization of expectations

School combines the expectations of the consumer expressed in
its claims with the beliefs of the producer expressed in its ritual.
It is a liturgical expression of a world-wide 'cargo cult', remi-
niscent of the cults which swept Melanesia in the 1940s, which
injected cultists with the belief that if they but put on a black
tie over their naked torsos, Jesus would arrive in a steamer bear-
ing an icebox, a pair of trousers and a sewing machine for each
believer.

School fuses the growth in humiliating dependence on a
master with the growth in the futile sense of omnipotence that
is so typical of the pupil who wants to go out and teach all nations to save themselves. The ritual is tailored to the stern work
habits of the hardhats, and its purpose is to celebrate the myth
of an earthly paradise of never-ending consumption, which is
the only hope for the wretched and dispossessed.

Epidemics of insatiable this-worldly expectations have occur-
red throughout history, especially among colonized and marginal groups in all cultures. Jews in the Roman Empire had
their Essenes and Jewish messiahs, serfs in the Reformation
their Thomas Münzer, dispossessed Indians from Paraguay to
Dakota their infectious dancers. These sects were always led by
a prophet, and limited their promises to a chosen few. The
school-induced expectation of the kingdom, on the other hand,
is impersonal rather than prophetic, and universal rather than
local. Man has become the engineer of his own messiah and
promises the unlimited rewards of science to those who submit
to progressive engineering for his reign.

The new alienation

School is not only the New World Religion. It is also the world's
fastest-growing labour market. The engineering of consumers
has become the economy's principal growth sector. As production
costs decrease in rich nations, there is an increasing concentration of both capital and labour in the vast enterprise of equipping

man for disciplined consumption. During the past decade capital investments directly related to the school system rose even faster than expenditures for defence. Disarmament would only accelerate the process by which the learning industry moves to the centre of the national economy. School gives unlimited opportunity for legitimated waste, so long as its destructiveness goes unrecognized and the cost of palliatives goes up.

If we add those engaged in full-time teaching to those in full-time attendance, we realize that this so-called superstructure has become society's major employer. In the United States sixty-two million people are in school and eighty million at work elsewhere. This is often forgotten by neo-Marxist analysts who say that the process of deschooling must be postponed or bracketed until other disorders, traditionally understood as more fundamental, are corrected by an economic and political revolution. Only if school is understood as an industry can revolutionary strategy be planned realistically. For Marx, the cost of producing demands for commodities was barely significant. Today most human labour is engaged in the production of demands that can be satisfied by industry which makes intensive use of capital. Most of this is done in school.

Alienation, in the traditional scheme, was a direct consequence of work's becoming wage-labour which deprived man of the opportunity to create and be recreated. Now young people are pre-alienated by schools that isolate them while they pretend to be both producers and consumers of their own knowledge, which is conceived of as a commodity put on the market in school. School makes alienation preparatory to life, thus depriving education of reality and work of creativity. School prepares for the alienating institutionalization of life by teaching the need to be taught. Once this lesson is learned, people lose their incentive to grow in independence; they no longer find relatedness attractive, and close themselves off to the surprises which life offers when it is not predetermined by institutional definition. And school directly or indirectly employs a major portion of the population. School either keeps people for life or makes sure that they will fit into some institution.

The New World Church is the knowledge industry, both purveyor of opium and the workbench during an increasing number of the years of an individual's life. Deschooling is, therefore, at the root of any movement for human liberation.

The revolutionary potential of deschooling

Of course, school is not, by any means, the only modern institution which has as its primary purpose the shaping of man's vision of reality. The hidden curriculum of family life, draft, health care, so-called professionalism, or of the media play an important part in the institutional manipulation of man's world – vision, language and demands. But school enslaves more profoundly and more systematically, since only school is credited with the principal function of forming critical judgement, and, paradoxically, tries to do so by making learning about oneself, about others, and about nature depend on a prepackaged process. School touches us so intimately that none of us can expect to be liberated from it by something else.

Many self-styled revolutionaries are victims of school. They see even 'liberation' as the product of an institutional process. Only liberating oneself from school will dispel such illusions. The discovery that most learning requires no teaching can be neither manipulated nor planned. Each of us is personally responsible for his or her own deschooling, and only we have the power to do it. No one can be excused if he fails to liberate himself from schooling. People could not free themselves from the Crown until at least some of them had freed themselves from the established Church. They cannot free themselves from progressive consumption until they free themselves from obligatory school.

We are all involved in schooling, from both the side of production and that of consumption. We are superstitiously convinced that good learning can and should be produced in us – and that we can produce it in others. Our attempt to withdraw from the concept of school will reveal the resistance we find in ourselves when we try to renounce limitless consumption and the pervasive presumption that others can be manipulated for their own good. No one is fully exempt from the exploitation of others in the schooling process.

School is both the largest and the most anonymous employer of all. Indeed, the school is the best example of a new kind of enterprise, succeeding the guild, the factory and the corporation. The multinational corporations which have dominated the economy are now being complemented, and may one day be replaced, by supernationally planned service agencies. These enterprises present their services in ways that make all men feel obliged to consume them. They are internationally standardized, redefining the value of their services periodically and everywhere at approximately the same rhythm.

'Transportation' relying on new cars and superhighways serves the same institutionally packaged need for comfort, prestige, speed and gadgetry, whether its components are produced by the state or not. The apparatus of 'medical care' defines a peculiar kind of health, whether the service is paid for by the state or by the individual. Graded promotion in order to obtain diplomas fits the student for a place on the same international pyramid of qualified manpower, no matter who directs the school.

In all these cases employment is a hidden benefit: the driver of a private car, the patient who submits to hospitalization, or the pupil in the schoolroom must now be seen as part of a new class of 'employees'. A liberation movement which starts in school, and yet is grounded in the awareness of teachers and pupils as simultaneously exploiters and exploited, could foreshadow the revolutionary strategies of the future; for a radical programme of deschooling could train youth in the new style of revolution needed to challenge a social system featuring obligatory 'health', 'wealth' and 'security'.

The risks of a revolt against school are unforeseeable, but they are not as horrible as those of a revolution starting in any other major institution. School is not yet organized for self-protection as effectively as a nation-state, or even a large corporation. Liberation from the grip of schools could be bloodless. The weapons of the truant officer and his allies in the courts and employment agencies might take very cruel measures against the individual offender, especially if he or she were poor, but they might turn out to be powerless against the surge of a mass movement.

School has become a social problem; it is being attacked on all sides, and citizens and their governments sponsor unconventional experiments all over the world. They resort to unusual statistical devices in order to keep faith and save face. The mood among some educators is much like the mood among Catholic bishops after the Vatican Council. The curricula of so-called 'free schools' resemble the liturgies of folk and rock masses. The demands of high-school students to have a say in choosing their teachers are as strident as those of parishioners demanding to select their pastors. But the stakes for society are much higher if a significant minority loses its faith in schooling. This would endanger the survival not only of the economic order built on the coproduction of goods and demands, but equally of the political order built on the nation-state into which students are delivered by the school.

Our options are clear enough. Either we continue to believe that institutionalized learning is a product which justifies unlimited investment, or we rediscover that legislation and planning and investment, if they have any place in formal education, should be used mostly to tear down the barriers that now impede opportunities for learning, which can only be a personal activity.

If we do not challenge the assumption that valuable knowledge is a commodity which under certain circumstances may be forced into the consumer, society will be increasingly dominated by sinister pseudo schools and totalitarian managers of information. Pedagogical therapists will drug their pupils more in order to teach them better, and students will drug themselves more to gain relief from the pressures of teachers and the race for certificates. Increasingly larger numbers of bureaucrats will presume to pose as teachers. The language of the schoolman has already been coopted by the adman. Now the general and the policeman try to dignify their professions by masquerading as educators. In a schooled society, war-making and civil repression find an educational rationale. Pedagogical warfare in the style of Vietnam will be increasingly justified as the only way of teaching people the superior value of unending progress.

Repression will be seen as a missionary effort to hasten the coming of the mechanical messiah. More and more countries will resort to the pedagogical torture already implemented in Brazil and Greece. This pedagogical torture is not used to extract information or to satisfy the psychic needs of sadists. It relies on random terror to break the integrity of an entire population and make it plastic material for the teachings invented by technocrats. The totally destructive and constantly progressive nature of obligatory instruction will fulfil its ultimate logic unless we begin to liberate ourselves right now from our pedagogical hubris, our belief that man can do what God cannot, namely, manipulate others for their own salvation.

Many people are just awakening to the inexorable destruction which present production trends imply for the environment, but individuals have only very limited power to change these trends. The manipulation of men and women begun in school has also reached a point of no return, and most people are still unaware of it. They still encourage school reform, as Henry Ford III proposes less poisonous cars.

Daniel Bell says that our epoch is characterized by an extreme disjunction between cultural and social structures, the one being devoted to apocalyptic attitudes, the other to technocratic decision-making. This is certainly true for many educational reformers, who feel impelled to condemn almost everything which characterizes modern schools – and at the same time propose new schools.

In his *The Structure of Scientific Revolution*, Thomas Kuhn argues that such dissonance inevitably precedes the emergence of a new cognitive paradigm. The facts reported by those who observed free fall, by those who returned from the other side of the earth, and by those who used the new telescope did not fit the Ptolemaic world view. Quite suddenly, the Newtonian paradigm was accepted. The dissonance which characterizes many of the young today is not so much cognitive as a matter of attitudes – a feeling about what a tolerable society can*not* be like. What is surprising about this dissonance is the ability of a very large number of people to tolerate it.

The capacity to pursue incongruous goals requires an explanation. According to Max Gluckman, all societies have procedures to hide such dissonances from their members. He suggests that this is the purpose of ritual. Rituals can hide from their participants even discrepancies and conflicts between social principle and social organization. As long as an individual is not explicitly conscious of the ritual character of the process through which he was initiated to the forces which shape his cosmos, he cannot break the spell and shape a new cosmos. As long as we are not aware of the ritual through which school shapes the progressive consumer – the economy's major resource – we cannot break the spell of this economy and shape a new one.

4 Institutional Spectrum

Most utopian schemes and futuristic scenarios call for new and costly technologies, which would have to be sold to rich and poor nations alike. Herman Kahn has found pupils in Venezuela, Argentina, and Colombia. The pipe dreams of Sergio Bernardes for his Brazil of the year 2000 sparkle with more new machinery than is now possessed by the United States, which by then will be weighted down with the antiquated missile sites, jetports and cities of the 1960s and 1970s. Futurists inspired by Buckminster Fuller would depend on cheaper and more exotic devices. They count on the acceptance of a new but possible technology that would apparently allow us to make more with less – lightweight monorails rather than supersonic transport; vertical living rather than horizontal sprawling. All of today's futuristic planners seek to make economically feasible what is technically possible while refusing to face the inevitable social consequence: the increased craving of all men for goods and services that will remain the privilege of a few.

I believe that a desirable future depends on our deliberately choosing a life of action over a life of consumption, on our engendering a life-style which will enable us to be spontaneous, independent, yet related to each other, rather than maintaining a life-style which only allows us to make and unmake, produce and consume – a style of life which is merely a way station on the road to the depletion and pollution of the environment. The future depends more upon our choice of institutions which support a life of action than on our developing new ideologies and technologies. We need a set of criteria which will permit us to recognize those institutions which support personal growth rather than addiction, as well as the will to invest our technological resources preferentially in such institutions of growth.

The choice is between two radically opposed institutional types, both of which are exemplified in certain existing institutions, although one type so characterizes the contemporary period as to almost define it. This dominant type I would propose to call the manipulative institution. The other type also exists, but only precariously. The institutions which fit it are humbler and less noticeable; yet I take them as models for a more desirable future. I call them 'convivial' and suggest placing them at the left of an institutional spectrum, both to show that there are institutions which fall between the extremes and to illustrate how historical institutions can change colour as they shift from facilitating activity to organizing production.

Generally, such a spectrum, moving from left to right, has been used to characterize men and their ideologies, not our social institutions and their styles. This categorization of men, whether as individuals or in groups, often generates more heat than light. Weighty objections can be raised against using an ordinary convention in an unusual fashion, but by doing so I hope to shift the terms of the discussion from a sterile to a fertile plane. It will become evident that men of the left are not always characterized by their opposition to the manipulative institutions, which I locate to the right on the spectrum.

The most influential modern institutions crowd up at the right of the spectrum. Law enforcement has moved there, as it has shifted from the hands of the sheriff to those of the FBI and the Pentagon. Modern warfare has become a highly professional enterprise whose business is killing. It has reached the point where its efficiency is measured in body counts. Its peace-keeping potential depends on its ability to convince friend and foe of the nation's unlimited death-dealing power. Modern bullets and chemicals are so effective that a few cents' worth, properly delivered to the intended 'client', unfailingly kill or maim. But delivery costs rise vertiginously; the cost of a dead Vietnamese went from $360,000 in 1967 to $450,000 in 1969. Only economies on a scale approaching race suicide would render modern warfare economically efficient. The boomerang effect in war is becoming more obvious: the higher the body count of dead Vietnamese, the more enemies the United States acquires around the world; likewise, the more the United States must spend to create another manipulative institution – cynically dubbed 'pacification' – in a futile effort to absorb the side-effects of war.

At this same extreme on the spectrum we also find social agencies which specialize in the manipulation of their clients. Like the military, they tend to develop effects contrary to their aims as the scope of their operations increases. These social institutions are equally counter-productive, but less obviously so. Many assume a therapeutic and compassionate image to mask this paradoxical effect. For example, gaols, up until two centuries ago, served as a means of detaining men until they were sentenced, maimed, killed or exiled, and were sometimes deliberately used as a form of torture. Only recently have we begun to claim that locking people up in cages will have a beneficial effect on their character and behaviour. Now quite a few people are beginning to understand that gaol increases both the quality and the quantity of criminals, that, in fact, it often creates them out of mere non-conformists. Far fewer people, however, seem to understand that mental hospitals, nursing homes and orphan asylums do much the same thing. These institutions provide their clients with the destructive self-image of the psychotic, the over-aged or the waif, and provide a rationale for the existence of entire professions, just as gaols produce income for wardens. Membership in the institutions found at this extreme of the spectrum is achieved in two ways, both coercive: by forced commitment or by selective service.

At the opposite extreme of the spectrum lie institutions distinguished by spontaneous use – the 'convivial' institutions. Telephone link-ups, subway lines, mail routes, public markets and exchanges do not require hard or soft sells to induce their clients to use them. Sewage systems, drinking water, parks and sidewalks are institutions men use without having to be institutionally convinced that it is to their advantage to do so. Of course, all institutions require some regulation. But the operation of institutions which exist to be used rather than to produce something requires rules of an entirely different nature from those required by treatment-institutions, which are manipulative. The rules which govern institutions for use have mainly the purpose of avoiding abuses which would frustrate their general accessibility. Pavements must be kept free of obstructions, the industrial use of drinking water must be held within limits, and ball playing must be restricted to special areas within a park. At present we need legislation to limit the abuse of our telephone lines by computers, the abuse of mail service by advertisers and the pollution of our sewage systems by industrial wastes. The regulation of convivial institutions sets limits to their use; as one moves from the convivial to the manipulative end of the spectrum, the rules progressively call for unwilling consumption or participation. The different cost of acquiring clients is just one of the characteristics which distinguish convivial from manipulative institutions.

At both extremes of the spectrum we find service institutions, but on the right the service is imposed manipulation, and the client is made the victim of advertising, aggression, indoctrination, imprisonment or electro-shock. On the left the service is amplified opportunity within formally defined limits, while the client remains a free agent. Right-wing institutions tend to be highly complex and costly production processes in which much of the elaboration and expense is concerned with convincing consumers that they cannot live without the product or the treatment offered by the institution. Left-wing institutions tend to be networks which facilitate client-initiated communication or cooperation.

The manipulative institutions of the right are either socially or psychologically 'addictive'. Social addiction, or escalation, consists in the tendency to prescribe increased treatment if smaller quantities have not yielded the desired results. Psychological addiction, or habituation, results when consumers become hooked on the need for more and more of the process or product. The self-activated institutions of the left tend to be self-limiting. Unlike production processes which identify satisfaction with the mere act of consumption, these networks serve a purpose beyond their own repeated use. An individual picks up the telephone when he wants to say something to someone else, and hangs up when the desired communication is over. He does not, teenagers excepted, use the telephone for the sheer pleasure of talking into the receiver. If the telephone is not the best way to get in touch, people will write a letter or take a trip. Right-wing institutions, as we can see clearly in the case of schools, both

invite compulsively repetitive use and frustrate alternative ways
of achieving similar results.

Towards, but not at, the left on the institutional spectrum,
we can locate enterprises which compete with others in their
own field, but have not begun notably to engage in advertising.
Here we find hand laundries, small bakeries, hairdressers, and –
to speak of professionals – some lawyers and music teachers.
Characteristically left of centre, then, are self-employed persons
who have institutionalized their services but not their publicity.
They acquire clients through their personal touch and the com-
parative quality of their services.

Hotels and cafeterias are somewhat closer to the centre. The
big chains like Hilton – which spend huge amounts on selling
their image – often behave as if they were running institutions
of the right. Yet Hilton and Sheraton enterprises do not usually
offer anything more – in fact, they often give less – than similarly priced, independently managed lodgings. Essentially, a hotel sign beckons to a traveller in the manner of a road sign. It
says, 'Stop, here is a bed for you', rather than, 'You should
prefer a hotel bed to a park bench!'

The producers of staples and most perishable consumer goods
belong in the middle of our spectrum. They fill generic demands
and add to the cost of production and distribution whatever the
market will bear in advertising costs for publicity and special
packaging. The more basic the product

ndom terror to break the integrity of an entire popu-
make it plastic material for the teachings invented by
s. The totally destructive and constantly progressive
obligatory instruction will fulfil its ultimate logic un-
gin to liberate ourselves right now from our pedagogical
ur belief that man can do what God cannot, namely,
te others for their own salvation.

people are just awakening to the inexorable destruction
resent production trends imply for the environment,
viduals have only very limited power to change these
The manipulation of men and women begun in school
reached a point of no return, and most people are still
e of it. They still encourage school reform, as Henry
II proposes less poisonous cars.

iel Bell says that our epoch is characterized by an extreme
ction between cultural and social structures, the one being
d to apocalyptic attitudes, the other to technocratic deci-
naking. This is certainly true for many educational re-
rs, who feel impelled to condemn almost everything which
cterizes modern schools – and at the same time propose
schools.

his The Structure of Scientific Revolution, Thomas Kuhn
es that such dissonance inevitably precedes the emergence
new cognitive paradigm. The facts reported by those who
rved free fall, by those who returned from the other side of
earth, and by those who used the new telescope did not fit
Ptolemaic world view. Quite suddenly, the Newtonian para-
m was accepted. The dissonance which characterizes many
the young today is not so much cognitive as a matter of atti-
des – a feeling about what a tolerable society cannot be like.
hat is surprising about this dissonance is the ability of a very
rge number of people to tolerate it.

The capacity to pursue incongruous goals requires an explana-
ion. According to Max Gluckman, all societies have procedures
o hide such dissonances from their members. He suggests that
this is the purpose of ritual. Rituals can hide from their participants even discrepancies and conflicts between social principle
and social organization. As long as an individual is not explicitly
conscious of the ritual character of the process through which he

lobbyists. The list price includes souped-up engines, air-conditioning, safety belts and exhaust controls; but other costs not openly declared to the driver are also involved: the corporation's advertising and sales expenses, fuel, maintenance and parts, insurance, interest on credit, as well as less tangible costs like loss of time, temper and breathable air in our traffic-congested cities.

An especially interesting corollary to our discussion of socially useful institutions is the system of 'public' highways. This major element of the total cost of cars deserves lengthier treatment, since it leads directly to the rightist institution in which I am most interested, namely, the school.

False public utilities

The highway system is a network for locomotion across relatively large distances. As a network, it appears to belong on the left of the institutional spectrum. But here we must make a distinction which will clarify both the nature of highways and the nature of true public utilities. Genuinely all-purpose roads are true public utilities. Superhighways are private preserves, the cost of which has been partially foisted upon the public.

Telephone, postal and highway systems are all networks, and none of them is free. Access to the telephone network is limited by time charges on each call. These rates are relatively small and could be reduced without changing the nature of the system. Use of the telephone system is not in the least limited by what is transmitted, although it is best used by those who can speak coherent sentences in the language of the other party – an ability universally possessed by those who wish to use the network. Postage is usually cheap. Use of the postal system is slightly limited by the price of pen and paper, and somewhat more by the ability to write. Still, when someone who does not know how to write has a relative or friend to whom he can dictate a letter, the postal system is at his service, as it is if he wants to ship a recorded tape.

The highway system does not similarly become available to someone who merely learns to drive. The telephone and postal networks exist to serve those who wish to use them, while the highway system mainly serves as an accessory to the private car.

The former are true public utilities, whereas the latter is a public service to the owners of cars, lorries and buses. Public utilities exist for the sake of communication among men; highways, like other institutions of the right, exist for the sake of a product. Car manufacturers, we have already observed, *produce* simultaneously both cars and the demand for cars. They also *produce* the demand for multi-lane highways, bridges and oilfields. The private car is the focus of a cluster of right-wing institutions. The high cost of each element is dictated by elaboration of the basic product, and to sell the basic product is to 'hook' society on the entire package.

To plan a highway system as a true public utility would discriminate against those for whom velocity and individualized comfort are the primary transportation values, in favour of those who value fluidity and destination. It is the difference between a far-flung network with maximum access for travellers and one which offers only privileged access to restricted areas.

Transferring a modern institution to the developing nations provides the acid test of its quality. In very poor countries roads are usually just good enough to permit transit by special, high-axle trucks loaded with groceries, livestock or people. This kind of country should use its limited resources to build a spiderweb of trails extending to every region and should restrict imports to two or three different models of highly durable vehicles which can manage all trails at low speed. This would simplify maintenance and the stocking of spare parts, permit the operation of these vehicles around the clock and provide maximum fluidity and choice of destination to all citizens. This would require the engineering of all-purpose vehicles with the simplicity of the Model T, making use of the most modern alloys to guarantee durability, with a built-in speed limit of not more than fifteen miles per hour, and strong enough to run on the roughest terrain. Such vehicles are not on the market because there is no demand for them. As a matter of fact, such a demand would have to be cultivated, quite possibly under the protection of strict legislation. At present, whenever such a demand is even slightly felt, it is quickly snuffed out by counter-publicity aimed at universal sales of the machines which currently extract from US taxpayers the money needed for building superhighways.

In order to 'improve' transportation, all countries – even the poorest – now plan highway systems designed for the passenger cars and high-speed trailers which fit the velocity-conscious minority of producers and consumers in the elite classes. This approach is frequently rationalized as a saving of the most precious resource of a poor country: the time of the doctor, the school inspector or the public administrator. These men, of course, serve almost exclusively the same people who have, or hope one day to have, a car. Local taxes and scarce international exchange are wasted on *false public utilities*.

'Modern' technology transferred to poor countries falls into three large categories: goods, factories which make them, and service institutions – principally schools – which make men into modern producers and consumers. Most countries spend by far the largest proportion of their budget on schools. The school-made graduates then create a demand for other conspicuous utilities, such as industrial power, paved highways, modern hospitals and airports, and these in turn create a market for the goods made for rich countries and, after a while, the tendency to import obsolescent factories to produce them.

Of all 'false utilities', school is the most insidious. Highway systems produce only a demand for cars. Schools create a demand for the entire set of modern institutions which crowd the right end of the spectrum. A man who questioned the need for highways would be written off as a romantic; the man who questions the need for school is immediately attacked as either heartless or imperialist.

Schools as false public utilities

Like highways, schools, at first glance, give the impression of being equally open to all comers. They are, in fact, open only to those who consistently renew their credentials. Just as highways create the impression that their present level of cost per year is necessary if people are to move, so schools are presumed essential for attaining the competence required by a society which uses modern technology. We have exposed speedways as spurious public utilities by noting their dependence on private cars. Schools are based upon the equally spurious hypothesis that learning is the result of curricular teaching.

Highways result from a perversion of the desire and need for mobility into the demand for a private car. Schools themselves pervert the natural inclination to grow and learn into the demand for instruction. Demands for manufactured maturity is a far greater abnegation of self-initiated activity than the demand for manufactured goods. Schools are not only to the right of highways and cars; they belong near the extreme of the institutional spectrum occupied by total asylums. Even the producers of body counts kill only bodies. By making men abdicate the responsibility for their own growth, school leads many to a kind of spiritual suicide.

Highways are paid for in part by those who use them, since tolls and petrol taxes are extracted only from drivers. School, on the other hand, is a perfect system of regressive taxation, where the privileged graduates ride on the back of the entire paying public. School puts a head tax on promotion. The underconsumption of highway mileage is not nearly so costly as the underconsumption of schooling. The man who does not own a car in Los Angeles may be almost immobilized, but if he can somehow manage to reach a work place, he can get and hold a job. The school dropout has no alternative route. The suburbanite with his new Lincoln and his country cousin who drives a beat-up jalopy get essentially the same use out of the highway, even though one man's car costs thirty times more than the other's. The value of a man's schooling is a function of the number of years he has completed and of the costliness of the schools he has attended. The law compels no one to drive, whereas it obliges everyone to go to school.

The analysis of institutions according to their present placement on a left–right continuum enables me to clarify my belief that fundamental social change must begin with a change of consciousness about institutions and to explain why the dimension of a viable future turns on the rejuvenation of institutional style.

During the 1960s institutions born in different decades since the French Revolution simultaneously reached old age; public-school systems founded in the time of Jefferson or of Atatürk, along with others which started after the Second World War, all became bureaucratic, self-justifying and manipulative. The same thing happened to systems of social security, to labour unions, major churches and diplomacies, the care of the aged, and the disposal of the dead.

Today, for instance, the school systems of Colombia, Britain, the USSR and the US resemble each other more closely than US schools of the late 1890s resembled either today's or their contemporaries in Russia. Today all schools are obligatory, open-ended and competitive. The same convergence in institutional style affects health care, merchandising, personnel administration and political life. All these institutional processes tend to pile up at the manipulative end of the spectrum.

A merger of world bureaucracies results from this convergence of institutions. The style, the ranking systems and the paraphernalia (from textbook to computer) are standardized on the planning boards of Costa Rica or Afghanistan after the model of Western Europe.

Everywhere these bureaucracies seem to focus on the same task: promoting the growth of institutions of the right. They are concerned with the making of things, the making of ritual rules and the making – and reshaping – of 'executive truth', the ideology or fiat which establishes the current value which should be attributed to their product. Technology provides these bureaucracies with increasing power on the right hand of society. The left hand of society seems to wither, not because technology is less capable of increasing the range of human action, and providing time for the play of individual imagination and personal creativity, but because such use of technology does not increase the power of an elite which administers it. The postmaster has no control over the substantive use of the mails, the switchboard operator or Bell Telephone executive has no power to stop adultery, murder or subversion from being planned over his network.

At stake in the choice between the institutional right and left is the very nature of human life. Man must choose whether to be rich in things or in the freedom to use them. He must choose between alternate styles of life and related production schedules.

Aristotle had already discovered that 'making and acting' are different, so different, in fact, that one never includes the other. 'For neither is acting a way of making – nor making a way of truly acting. Architecture [*techne*] is a way of making ... of bringing something into being whose origin is in the maker and not in the thing. Making has always an end other than itself, action not; for good action itself is its end. Perfection in making is an art, perfection in acting is a virtue.'* The word which Aristotle employed for making was '*poesis*', and the word he employed for doing, '*praxis*'. A move to the right implies that an institution is being restructured to increase its ability to 'make', while as it moves to the left, it is being restructured to allow increased 'doing' or '*praxis*'. Modern technology has increased the ability of man to relinquish the 'making' of things to machines, and his potential time for 'acting' has increased. 'Making' the necessities of life has ceased to take up his time. Unemployment is the result of this modernization: it is the idleness of a man for whom there is nothing to 'make' and who does not know what to 'do' – that is, how to 'act'. Unemployment is the sad idleness of a man who, contrary to Aristotle, believes that making things, or working, is virtuous and that idleness is bad. Unemployment is the experience of the man who has succumbed to the Protestant ethic. Leisure, according to Weber, is necessary for man to be able to work. For Aristotle, work is necessary for man to have leisure.

Technology provides man with discretionary time he can fill either with making or with doing. The choice between sad unemployment and joyful leisure is now open for the entire culture. It depends on the institutional style the culture chooses. This choice would have been unthinkable in an ancient culture built either on peasant agriculture or on slavery. It has become inevitable for post-industrial man.

One way to fill available time is to stimulate increased demands for the consumption of goods and, simultaneously, for the production of services. The former implies an economy which provides an ever-growing array of ever newer things which can be made, consumed, wasted and recycled. The latter implies the futile attempt to 'make' virtuous actions into the products of 'service' institutions. This leads to the identification of schooling and education, of medical service and health, of programme-watching and entertainment, of speed and effective

*Nichomachean Ethics, 1140.

locomotion. This first option now goes under the name of development.

The radically alternative way to fill available time is a limited range of more durable goods and to provide access to institutions which can increase the opportunity and desirability of human interaction.

A durable-goods economy is precisely the contrary of an economy based on planned obsolescence. A durable-goods economy means a constraint on the bill of goods. Goods would have to be such that they provided the maximum opportunity to 'do' something with them: items made for self-assembly, self-help, re-use and repair.

The complement to a durable, repairable and re-usable bill of goods is not an increase of institutionally produced services, but rather an institutional framework which constantly educates to action, participation and self-help. The movement of our society from the present – in which all institutions gravitate towards post-industrial bureaucracy – to a future of post-industrial conviviality – in which the intensity of action would prevail over production – must begin with a renewal of style in the service institutions – and, first of all, with a renewal of education. A future which is desirable and feasible depends on our willingness to invest our technological know-how into the growth of convivial institutions. In the field of educational research, this amounts to the request for a reversal of present trends.

5 Irrational Consistencies*

I believe that the contemporary crisis of education demands that we review the very idea of publicly prescribed learning, rather than the methods used in its enforcement. The dropout rate – especially of junior-high-school students and elementary-school teachers – points to a grass-roots demand for a completely fresh look. The 'classroom practitioner' who considers himself a liberal teacher is increasingly attacked from all sides. The free-school movement, confusing discipline with indoctrination, has painted him into the role of a destructive authoritarian. The educational technologist consistently demonstrates the teacher's inferiority at measuring and modifying behaviour. And the school administration for which he works forces him to bow to both Summerhill and Skinner, making it obvious that compulsory learning cannot be a liberal enterprise. No wonder that the desertion rate of teachers is overtaking that of their students.

America's commitment to the compulsory education of its young now reveals itself to be as futile as the pretended American commitment to compulsory democratization of the Vietnamese. Conventional schools obviously cannot do it. The free-school movement entices unconventional educators, but ultimately does so in support of the conventional ideology of schooling. And the promises of educational technologists, that their research and development – if adequately funded – can offer some kind of final solution to the resistance of youth to compulsory learning, sound as confident and prove as fatuous as the analogous promises made by the military technologists.

The criticism directed at the American school system by the behaviourists and that coming from the new breed of radical

*This chapter was presented originally at a meeting of the American Educational Research Association, in New York City, 6 February 1971.

educators seem radically opposed. The behaviourists apply educational research to the 'induction of autotelic instruction through individualized learning packages'. Their style clashes with the non-directive cooption of youth into liberated communes established under the supervision of adults. Yet, in historical perspective, these two are just contemporary manifestations of the seemingly contradictory yet really complementary goals of the public-school system. From the beginning of this century, the schools have been protagonists of social control on the one hand and free cooperation on the other, both placed at the service of the 'good society', conceived of as a highly organized and smoothly working corporate structure. Under the impact of intense urbanization, children became a natural resource to be moulded by the schools and fed into the industrial machine. Progressive politics and the cult of efficiency converged in the growth of the US public school.* Vocational guidance and the junior high school were two important results of this kind of thinking.

It appears, therefore, that the attempt to produce specified behavioural changes which can be measured and for which the processor can be held accountable is just one side of a coin, whose other side is the pacification of the new generation within specially engineered enclaves which will seduce them into the dream world of their elders. These pacified in society are well described by Dewey, who wants us to 'make each one of our schools an embryonic community life, active with types of occupations that reflect the life of the larger society, and *permeate* it with the *spirit* of art, history and science'. In this historical perspective, it would be a grave mistake to interpret the current three-cornered controversy between the school establishment, the educational technologists and the free schools as the prelude to a revolution in education. This controversy reflects rather a stage of an attempt to escalate an old dream into fact, and to finally make all valuable learning the result of professional teaching. Most educational alternatives proposed converge towards goals which are immanent in the production of the cooperative man whose individual needs are met by means

*See Joel Spring, *Education and the Rise of the Corporate State*, CIDOC document no. 50, Cuernavaca, Mexico, 1971.

of his specialization in the American system: they are oriented towards the improvement of what – for lack of a better phrase – I call the schooled society. Even the seemingly radical critics of the school system are not willing to abandon the idea that they have an obligation to the young, especially to the poor, an obligation to process them, whether by love or by fear, into a society which needs disciplined specialization as much from its producers as from its consumers and also their full commitment to the ideology which puts economic growth first.

Dissent veils the contradictions inherent in the very idea of school. The established teachers' unions, the technological wizards and the educational liberation movement reinforce the commitment of the entire society to the fundamental axioms of a schooled world, somewhat in the manner in which many peace and protest movements reinforce the commitments of their members – be they black, female, young or poor – to seek justice through the growth of the gross national income.

Some of the tenets which now go unchallenged are easy to list. There is, first, the shared belief that behaviour which has been acquired in the sight of a pedagogue is of special value to the pupil and of special benefit to society. This is related to the assumption that social man is born only in adolescence, and properly born only if he matures in the school-womb, which some want to gentle by permissiveness, others to stuff with gadgets and still others to varnish with a liberal tradition. And there is, finally, a shared view of youth which is psychologically romantic and politically conservative. According to this view, changes in society must be brought about by burdening the young with the responsibility of transforming it – but only after their eventual release from school. It is easy for a society founded on such tenets to build up a sense of its responsibility for the education of the new generation, and this inevitably means that some men may set, specify and evaluate the personal goals of others. In a 'passage from an imaginary Chinese encyclopedia', Jorge Luis Borges tries to evoke the sense of giddiness such an attempt must produce. He tells us that animals are divided into the following classes: '(a) those belonging to the emperor, (b) those that are embalmed, (c) those that are domesticated, (d) the suckling pigs, (e) the sirens, (f) fabulous ones, (g) the roaming dogs, (h) those included in the present classification, (i) those that drive themselves crazy, (j) innumerable ones, (k) those painted with a very fine brush of camel hair, (l) et cetera, (m) those who have just broken the jug, (n) those who resemble flies from afar.' Now, such a taxonomy does not come into being unless somebody feels it can serve his purpose: in this case, I suppose, that somebody was a tax collector. For him, at least, this taxonomy of beasts *must* have made sense, the same way in which the taxonomy of educational objectives makes sense to scientific authors.

In the peasant, the vision of men with such inscrutable logic, empowered to assess his cattle, must have induced a chilling sense of impotence. Students, for analogous reasons, tend to feel paranoiac when they seriously submit to a curriculum. Inevitably they are even more frightened than my imaginary Chinese peasant, because it is their life-goals rather than their lifestock which is being branded with an inscrutable sign.

This passage of Borges is fascinating, because it evokes the logic of *irrational consistency* which makes Kafka's and Koestler's bureaucracies so sinister yet so evocative of everyday life. Irrational consistency mesmerizes accomplices who are engaged in mutually expedient and disciplined exploitation. It is the logic generated by bureaucratic behaviour. And it becomes the logic of a society which demands that the managers of its educational institutions be held publicly accountable for the behavioural modification they produce in their clients. Students who can be motivated to value the educational packages which their teachers obligate them to consume are comparable to Chinese peasants who can fit their flocks into the tax form provided by Borges.

At some time during the last two generations a commitment to therapy triumphed in American culture, and teachers came to be regarded as the therapists whose ministrations all men need, if they wish to enjoy the equality and freedom with which, according to the Constitution, they are born. Now the teacher-therapists go on to propose life-long educational treatment as the next step. The *style* of this treatment is under discussion: Should it take the form of continued adult classroom attendance? Electronic ecstasy? Or periodic sensitivity sessions? All educators are ready to conspire to push out the walls of the classroom, with the goal of transforming the entire culture into a school.

The American controversy over the future of education, behind its rhetoric and noise, is more conservative than the discourse in other areas of public policy. On foreign affairs, at least, an organized minority constantly reminds us that the United States must renounce its role as the world's policeman. Radical economists, and now even their less radical teachers, question aggregate growth as a desirable goal. There are lobbies for prevention over cure in medicine and others in favour of fluidity over speed in transportation. Only in the field of education do the articulate voices demanding a radical deschooling of society remain so dispersed. There is a lack of cogent argument and of mature leadership aiming at the disestablishment of any and all institutions which serve the purpose of compulsory *learning*. For a moment, the radical deschooling of society is still a cause without a party. This is especially surprising in a time of growing, though chaotic, resistance to all forms of institutionally planned instruction on the part of those aged twelve to seventeen.

Educational innovators still assume that educational institutions function like funnels for the programmes they package. For my argument it is irrelevant whether these funnels take the form of a classroom, a TV transmitter or a 'liberated zone'. It is equally irrelevant whether the packages purveyed are rich or poor, hot or cold, hard and measurable (like Maths III), or impossible to assess (like sensitivity). What counts is that education is assumed to be the result of an institutional process managed by the educator. As long as the relations continue to be those between a supplier and a consumer, educational research will remain a circular process. It will amass scientific evidence in support of the need for more educational packages and for their more deadly accurate delivery to the individual customer, just as a certain brand of social science can prove the need for the delivery of more military treatment.

An educational revolution depends on a twofold inversion: a new orientation for research and a new understanding of the educational style of an emerging counter-culture.

Operational research now seeks to optimize the efficiency of an inherited framework – a framework which is itself never questioned. This framework has the syntactic structure of a funnel for teaching packages. The syntactic alternative to it is an educational network or web for the autonomous assembly of resources under the personal control of each learner. This alternative structure of an educational institution now lies within the conceptual blindspot of our operational research. If research were to focus on it, this would constitute a true scientific revolution.

The blindspot of educational research reflects the cultural bias of a society in which technological growth has been confused with technocratic control. For the technocrat the value of an environment increases as more contacts between each man and his milieu can be programmed. In this world the choices which are manageable for the observer or planner converge with the choices possible for the observed so-called beneficiary. Freedom is reduced to a selection among packaged commodities.

The emerging counter-culture reaffirms the values of semantic content above the efficiency of increased and more rigid syntax. It values the wealth of connotation above the power of syntax to produce wealth. It values the unpredictable outcome of self-chosen personal encounter above the certified quality of professional instruction. This reorientation towards personal surprise rather than institutionally engineered values will be disruptive of the established order until we dissociate the increasing availability of technological tools which facilitate encounter from the increasing control of the technocrat of what happens when people meet.

Our present educational institutions are at the service of the teacher's goals. The relational structures we need are those which will enable each man to define himself by learning and by contributing to the learning of others.

6 Learning Webs

In a previous chapter I discussed what is becoming a common complaint about schools, one that is reflected, for example, in the recent report of the Carnegie Commission: in school registered students submit to certified teachers in order to obtain certificates of their own; both are frustrated and both blame insufficient resources – money, time or buildings – for their mutual frustration.

Such criticism leads many people to ask whether it is possible to conceive of a different style of learning. The same people, paradoxically, when pressed to specify how they acquired what they know and value, will readily admit that they learned it more often outside than inside school. Their knowledge of facts, their understanding of life and work came to them from friendship or love, while viewing TV, or while reading, from examples of peers or the challenge of a street encounter. Or they may have learned what they know through the apprenticeship ritual for admission to a street gang or the initiation to a hospital, newspaper city room, plumber's shop or insurance office. The alternative to dependence on schools is not the use of public resources for some new device which 'makes' people learn; rather it is the creation of a new style of educational relationship between man and his environment. To foster this style, attitudes towards growing up, the tools available for learning, and the quality and structure of daily life will have to change concurrently.

Attitudes are already changing. The proud dependence on school is gone. Consumer resistance increases in the knowledge industry. Many teachers and pupils, taxpayers and employers, economists and policemen would prefer not to depend any longer on schools. What prevents their frustration from shaping

new institutions is a lack not only of imagination but frequently
also of appropriate language and of enlightened self-interest.
They cannot visualize either a deschooled society or educational
institutions in a society which has disestablished school.

In this chapter I intend to show that the inverse of school is
possible: that we can depend on self-motivated learning instead
of employing teachers to bribe or compel the student to find the
time and the will to learn; that we can provide the learner with
new links to the world instead of continuing to funnel all educational programmes through the teacher. I shall discuss some
of the general characteristics which distinguish schooling from
learning and outline four major categories of educational institutions which should appeal not only to many individuals
but also to many existing interest groups.

An objection: who can be served by bridges to nowhere?

We are used to considering schools as a variable, dependent on
the political and economic structure. If we can change the style
of political leadership, or promote the interests of one class or
another, or switch from private to public ownership of the
means of production, we assume the school system will change
as well. The educational institutions I will propose, however,
are meant to serve a society which does not now exist, although
the current frustration with schools is itself potentially a major
force to set in motion change towards new social arrangements.
An obvious objection has been raised to this approach: why
channel energy to build bridges to nowhere, instead of marshal-
ling it first to change not the schools but the political and economic system?

This objection, however, underestimates the fundamental
political and economic nature of the school system itself, as
well as the political potential inherent in any effective challenge
to it.

In a basic sense, schools have ceased to be dependent on the
ideology professed by any government or market organization.
Other basic institutions might differ from one country to another: family, party, church or press. But everywhere the school
system has the same structure, and everywhere its hidden curriculum has the same effect. Invariably, it shapes the consumer

who values institutional commodities above the non-professional ministration of a neighbour.

Everywhere the hidden curriculum of schooling initiates the citizen to the myth that bureaucracies guided by scientific knowledge are efficient and benevolent. Everywhere this same curriculum instils in the pupil the myth that increased production will provide a better life. And everywhere it develops the habit of self-defeating consumption of services and alienating production, the tolerance for institutional dependence, and the recognition of institutional rankings. The hidden curriculum of school does all this in spite of contrary efforts undertaken by teachers and no matter what ideology prevails.

In other words, schools are fundamentally alike in all countries, be they fascist, democratic or socialist, big or small, rich or poor. This identity of the school system forces us to recognize the profound world-wide identity of myth, mode of production and method of social control, despite the great variety of mythologies in which the myth finds expression.

In view of this identity, it is illusory to claim that schools are, in any profound sense, dependent variables. This means that to hope for fundamental change in the school system as an effect of conventionally conceived social or economic change is also an illusion. Moreover, this illusion grants the school – the reproductive organ of a consumer society – almost unquestioned immunity.

It is at this point that the example of China becomes important. For three millennia, China protected higher learning through a total divorce between the process of learning and the privilege conferred by mandarin examinations. To become a world power and a modern nation-state, China had to adopt the international style of schooling. Only hindsight will allow us to discover if the Great Cultural Revolution will turn out to have been the first successful attempt at deschooling the institutions of society.

Even the piecemeal creation of new educational agencies which were the inverse of school would be an attack on the most sensitive link of a pervasive phenomenon, which is organized by the state in all countries. A political programme which does not explicitly recognize the need for deschooling is not revolutionary;

it is demagoguery calling for more of the same. Any major political programme of the 1970s should be evaluated by this measure: how clearly does it state the need for deschooling – and how clearly does it provide guidelines for the educational quality of the society for which it aims?

The struggle against domination by the world market and big-power politics might be beyond some poor communities or countries, but this weakness is an added reason for emphasizing the importance of liberating each society through a reversal of its educational structure, a change which is not beyond any society's means.

General characteristics of
new formal educational institutions

A good educational system should have three purposes: it should provide all who want to learn with access to available resources at any time in their lives; empower all who want to share what they know to find those who want to learn it from them; and, finally, furnish all who want to present an issue to the public with the opportunity to make their challenge known. Such a system would require the application of constitutional guarantees to education. Learners should not be forced to submit to an obligatory curriculum, or to discrimination based on whether they possess a certificate or a diploma. Nor should the public be forced to support, through a regressive taxation, a huge professional apparatus of educators and buildings which in fact restricts the public's chances for learning to the services the profession is willing to put on the market. It should use modern technology to make free speech, free assembly and a free press truly universal and, therefore, fully educational.

Schools are designed on the assumption that there is a secret to everything in life; that the quality of life depends on knowing that secret; that secrets can be known only in orderly successions; and that only teachers can properly reveal these secrets. An individual with a schooled mind conceives of the world as a pyramid of classified packages accessible only to those who carry the proper tags. New educational institutions would break apart this pyramid. Their purpose must be to facilitate access for the learner: to allow him to look into the windows of the control room or the parliament, if he cannot get in by the door. Moreover, such new institutions should be channels to which the learner would have access without credentials or pedigree – public spaces in which peers and elders outside his immediate horizon would become available.

I believe that no more than four – possibly even three – distinct 'channels' or learning exchanges could contain all the resources needed for real learning. The child grows up in a world of things, surrounded by people who serve as models for skills and values. He finds peers who challenge him to argue, to compete, to cooperate and to understand; and if the child is lucky, he is exposed to confrontation or criticism by an experienced elder who really cares. Things, models, peers and elders are four resources each of which requires a different type of arrangement to ensure that everybody has ample access to it.

I will use the words 'opportunity web' for 'network' to designate specific ways to provide access to each of four sets of resources. 'Network' is often used, unfortunately, to designate the channels reserved to material selected by others for indoctrination, instruction and entertainment. But it can also be used for the telephone or the postal service, which are primarily accessible to individuals who want to send messages to one another. I wish we had another word to designate such reticular structures for mutual access, a word less evocative of entrapment, less degraded by current usage and more suggestive of the fact that any such arrangement includes legal, organizational and technical aspects. Not having found such a term, I will try to redeem the one which is available, using it as a synonym of 'educational web'.

What are needed are new networks, readily available to the public and designed to spread equal opportunity for learning and teaching.

To give an example: the same level of technology is used in TV and in tape recorders. All Latin American countries now have introduced TV: in Bolivia the government has financed a TV station, which was built six years ago, and there are no more than seven thousand TV sets for four million citizens. The money now tied up in TV installations throughout Latin America could have provided every fifth adult with a tape recorder. In addition, the money would have sufficed to provide an almost unlimited library of prerecorded tapes, with outlets even in remote villages, as well as an ample supply of empty tapes.

This network of tape recorders, of course, would be radically different from the present network of TV. It would provide opportunity for free expression: literate and illiterate alike could record, preserve, disseminate and repeat their opinions. The present investment in TV, instead, provides bureaucrats, whether politicians or educators, with the power to sprinkle the continent with institutionally produced programmes which they – or their sponsors – decide are good for or in demand by the people.

Technology is available to develop either independence and learning or bureaucracy and teaching.

Four networks

The planning of new educational institutions ought not to begin with the administrative goals of a principal or president, or with the teaching goals of a professional educator, or with the learning goals of any hypothetical class of people. It must not start with the question, 'What should someone learn?' but with the question, 'What kinds of things and people might learners want to be in contact with in order to learn?'

Someone who wants to learn knows that he needs both information and critical response to its use from somebody else. Information can be stored in things and in persons. In a good educational system access to things ought to be available at the sole bidding of the learner, while access to informants requires, in addition, others' consent. Criticism can also come from two directions: from peers or from elders, that is, from fellow learners whose immediate interests match mine, or from those who will grant me a share in their superior experience. Peers can be colleagues with whom to raise a question, companions for playful and enjoyable (or arduous) reading or walking, challengers at any type of game. Elders can be consultants on which skill to learn, which method to use, what company to seek at a given moment. They can be guides to the right questions to be raised among peers and to the deficiency of the answers they arrive at. Most of these resources are plentiful. But they are neither conventionally perceived as educational resources, nor is access to them for learning purposes easy, especially for the poor. We must conceive of new relational structures which are deliberately set up to facilitate access to these resources for the use of anybody who is motivated to seek them for his education. Administrative, technological, and especially legal arrangements are required to set up such web-like structures.

Educational resources are usually labelled according to educators' curricular goals. I propose to do the contrary, to label four different approaches which enable the student to gain access to any educational resource which may help him to define and achieve his own goals:

1. Reference Services to Educational Objects – which facilitate access to things or processes used for formal learning. Some of these things can be reserved for this purpose, stored in libraries, rental agencies, laboratories and showrooms like museums and theatres; others can be in daily use in factories, airports or on farms, but made available to students as apprentices or on off-hours.

2. Skill Exchanges – which permit persons to list their skills, the conditions under which they are willing to serve as models for others who want to learn these skills, and the addresses at which they can be reached.

3. Peer-Matching – a communications network which permits persons to describe the learning activity in which they wish to engage, in the hope of finding a partner for the inquiry.

4. Reference Services to Educators-at-Large – who can be listed in a directory giving the addresses and self-descriptions of professionals, paraprofessionals and freelancers, along with conditions of access to their services. Such educators, as we will see, could be chosen by polling or consulting their former clients.

Reference services to educational objects

Things are basic resources for learning. The quality of the environment and the relationship of a person to it will determine how much he learns incidentally. Formal learning requires special access to ordinary things, on the one hand, or, on the other, easy and dependable access to special things made for educational purposes. An example of the former is the special right to operate or dismantle a machine in a garage. An example of the latter is the general right to use an abacus, a computer, a book, a botanical garden or a machine withdrawn from production and placed at the full disposal of students.

At present, attention is focused on the disparity between rich and poor children in their access to things and in the manner in which they can learn from them. The Office of Educational Opportunity and other agencies, following this approach, concentrate on equalizing chances, by trying to provide more educational equipment for the poor. A more radical point of departure would be to recognize that in the city rich and poor alike are artificially kept away from most of the things that surround them. Children born into the age of plastics and efficiency experts must penetrate two barriers which obstruct their understanding: one built into things and the other around institutions. Industrial design creates a world of things that resist insight into their nature, and schools shut the learner out of the world of things in their meaningful setting.

After a short visit to New York, a woman from a Mexican village told me she was impressed by the fact that stores sold 'only wares heavily made up with cosmetics'. I understood her to mean that industrial products 'speak' to their customers about their allurements and not about their nature. Industry has surrounded people with artifacts whose inner workings only specialists are allowed to understand. The non-specialist is discouraged from figuring out what makes a watch tick, or a telephone ring, or an electric typewriter work, by being warned that it will break if he tries. He can be told what makes a transistor radio work, but he cannot find out for himself. This type of design tends to reinforce a non-inventive society in which the experts find it progressively easier to hide behind their expertise and beyond evaluation.

The man-made environment has become as inscrutable as nature is for the primitive. At the same time, educational materials have been monopolized by school. Simple educational objects have been expensively packaged by the knowledge industry. They have become specialized tools for professional educators, and their cost has been inflated by forcing them to stimulate either environments or teachers.

The teacher is jealous of the textbook he defines as his professional implement. The student may come to hate the lab because he associates it with schoolwork. The administrator rationalizes his protective attitude towards the library as a defence of costly public equipment against those who would play with it rather than learn. In this atmosphere the student too often uses the map, the lab, the encyclopedia or the microscope only at the rare moments when the curriculum tells him to do so. Even the great classics become part of 'sophomore year' instead of marking a new turn in a person's life. School removes things from everyday use by labelling them education tools.

If we are to deschool, both tendencies must be reversed. The general physical environment must be made accessible, and those physical learning resources which have been reduced to teaching instruments must become generally available for self-directed learning. Using things only as part of a curriculum can have an even worse effect than just removing them from the general environment. It can corrupt the attitudes of pupils.

Games are a case in point. I do not mean the 'games' of the physical education department (such as football and basketball), which the schools use to raise income and prestige and in which they have made a substantial capital investment. As the athletes themselves are well aware, these enterprises, which take the form of warlike tournaments, have undermined the playfulness of sports and are used to reinforce the competitive nature of schools. Rather I have in mind the educational games which can provide a unique way to penetrate formal systems. Set theory, linguistics, propositional logic, geometry, physics and even chemistry reveal themselves with little effort to certain persons who play these games. A friend of mine went to a Mexican market with a game called 'Wff 'n Proof', which consists of some dice on which twelve logical symbols are imprinted. He showed children which two or three combinations constituted a well-formed sentence, and inductively within the first hour some onlookers also grasped the principle. Within a few hours of playfully conducting formal logical proofs, some children are capable of introducing others to the fundamental proofs of propositional logic. The others just walk away.

In fact, for some children such games are a special form of liberating education, since they heighten their awareness of the fact that formal systems are built on changeable axioms and that conceptual operations have a gamelike nature. They are also simple, cheap and – to a large extent – can be organized by the players themselves. Used outside the curriculum such games provide an opportunity for identifying and developing unusual talent, while the school psychologist will often identify those who have such talent as in danger of becoming anti-social, sick or unbalanced. Within school, when used in the form of tournaments, games are not only removed from the sphere of leisure; they often become tools used to translate playfulness into competition, a lack of abstract reasoning into a sign of inferiority. An exercise which is liberating for some character types becomes a straitjacket for others.

The control of school over educational equipment has still another effect. It increases enormously the cost of such cheap materials. Once their use is restricted to scheduled hours, professionals are paid to supervise their acquisition, storage and use. Then students vent their anger against the school on the equipment, which must be purchased once again.

Paralleling the untouchability of teaching tools is the impenetrability of modern junk. In the 1930s any self-respecting boy knew how to repair a car, but now car makers multiply wires and withhold manuals from everyone except specialized mechanics. In a former era an old radio contained enough coils and condensers to build a transmitter that would make all the neighbourhood radios scream in feedback. Transistor radios are more portable, but nobody dares to take them apart. To change this in the highly industrialized countries will be immensely difficult; but at least in the Third World we must insist on built-in educational qualities.

To illustrate my point, let me present a model: by spending ten million dollars it would be possible to connect forty thousand hamlets in a country like Peru with a spiderweb of six-foot-wide trails and maintain these, and, in addition, provide the country with 200,000 three-wheeled mechanical donkeys – five on the average for each hamlet. Few poor countries of this size spend less than this yearly on cars and roads, both of which are now restricted mainly to the rich and their employees, while poor people remain trapped in their villages. Each of these simple but durable little vehicles would cost $125 – half of which would pay for transmission and a six-horsepower motor. A 'donkey' could make 15 mph, and it can carry loads of 850 pounds (that is, most things besides tree trunks and steel beams which are ordinarily moved).

The political appeal of such a transportation system to a peasantry is obvious. Equally obvious is the reason why those who hold power – and thereby automatically have a car – are not interested in spending money on trails and in clogging roads with engine-driven donkeys. The universal donkey could work only if a country's leaders were willing to impose a national speed limit of, say, twenty-five miles an hour and adapt its public institutions to this. The model could not work if conceived only as a stopgap.

This is not the place to elaborate on the political, social, economic, financial and technical feasibility of this model. I wish only to indicate that educational considerations may be of prime importance when choosing such an alternative to capital-intensive transport. By raising the unit cost per donkey by some 20 per cent it would become possible to plan the production of all its parts in such a manner that, as far as possible, each future owner would spend a month or two making and understanding his machine and would be able to repair it. With this additional cost it would also be possible to decentralize production into dispersed plants. The added benefits would result not only from including educational costs in the construction process. Even more significantly, a durable motor which practically anyone could learn to repair and which could be used as a plough and pump by somebody who understood it would provide much higher educational benefits than the inscrutable engines of the advanced countries.

Not only the junk but also the supposedly public places of the modern city have become impenetrable. In American society, children are excluded from most things and places on the grounds that they are private. But even in societies which have declared an end to private property children are kept away from the same places and things because they are considered the special domain of professionals and dangerous to the uninitiated. Since the last generation the railroad yard has become as inaccessible as the fire station. Yet with a little ingenuity it should not be difficult to provide for safety in such places. To deschool the artifacts of education will require making the artifacts and processes available – and recognizing their educational value. Certainly, some workers would find it inconvenient to be accessible to learners; but this inconvenience must be balanced against the educational gains.

Private cars could be banned from Manhattan. Five years ago it was unthinkable. Now certain New York streets are closed off at odd hours, and this trend will probably continue. Indeed, most cross-streets should be closed to automotive traffic and parking should be forbidden everywhere. In a city opened up to people, teaching materials which are now locked up in storerooms and laboratories could be dispersed into independently operated storefront depots which children and adults could visit without the danger of being run over.

If the goals of learning were no longer dominated by schools and schoolteachers, the market for learners would be much more various and the definition of 'educational artifacts' would be less restrictive. There could be tool shops, libraries, laboratories and gaming rooms. Photo labs and offset presses would allow neighbourhood newspapers to flourish. Some storefront learning centres could contain viewing booths for closed-circuit television, others could feature office equipment for use and for repair. The jukebox or the record player would be commonplace, with some specializing in classical music, others in international folk tunes, others in jazz. Film clubs would compete with each other and with commercial television. Museum outlets could be networks for circulating exhibits of works of art, both old and new, originals and reproductions, perhaps administered by the various metropolitan museums.

The professional personnel needed for this network would be much more like custodians, museum guides or reference librarians than like teachers. From the corner biology store, they could refer their clients to the shell collection in the museum or indicate the next showing of biology videotapes in a certain viewing booth. They could furnish guides for pest control, diet and other kinds of preventive medicine. They could refer those who needed advice to 'elders' who could provide it.

Two distinct approaches can be taken to financing a network of 'learning objects'. A community could determine a. maximum budget for this purpose and arrange for all parts of the network to be open to all visitors at reasonable hours. Or the community could decide to provide citizens with limited entitlements, according to their age group, which would give them special access to certain materials which are both costly and scarce, while leaving other, simpler materials available to everyone.

Finding resources for materials made specifically for education is only one – and perhaps the least costly – aspect of building an educational world. The money now spent on the sacred paraphernalia of the school ritual could be freed to provide all citizens with greater access to the real life of the city. Special tax incentives could be granted to those who employed children between the ages of eight and fourteen for a couple of hours each day if the conditions of employment were humane ones. We should return to the tradition of the *barmitzvah* or confirmation. By this I mean we should first restrict, and later eliminate, the disenfranchizement of the young and permit a boy of twelve to become a man fully responsible for his participation in the life of the community. Many 'school-age' people know more about their neighbourhood than social workers or councilmen. Of course, they also ask more embarrassing questions and propose solutions which threaten the bureaucracy. They should be allowed to come of age so that they could put their knowledge and fact-finding ability to work in the service of a popular government.

Until recently the dangers of school were easily underestimated in comparison with the dangers of an apprenticeship in the police force, the fire department or the entertainment industry. It was easy to justify schools at least as a means to protect youth. Often this argument no longer holds. I recently visited a Methodist church in Harlem occupied by a group of armed

Young Lords in protest against the death of Julio Rodan, a Puerto Rican youth found hanged in his prison cell. I knew the leaders of the group who had spent a semester in Cuernavaca. When I wondered why one of them, Juan, was not among them, I was told that he had 'gone back on heroin and to the State University'.

Planning, incentives and legislation can be used to unlock the educational potential within our society's huge investment in plants and equipment. Full access to educational objects will not exist so long as business firms are allowed to combine the legal protections which the Bill of Rights reserves to the privacy of individuals with the economic power conferred upon them by their millions of customers and thousands of employees, stockholders and suppliers. Much of the world's know-how and most of its productive processes and equipment are locked within the walls of business firms, away from their customers, employees and stockholders, as well as from the general public, whose laws and facilities allow them to function. Money now spent on advertising in capitalist countries could be redirected towards education in and by General Electric, NBC-TV or Budweiser beer. That is, the plants and offices should be reorganized so that their daily operations could be more accessible to the public in ways that would make learning possible; and, indeed, ways might be found to pay the companies for the learning people acquired from them.

An even more valuable body of scientific objects and data may be withheld from general access – and even from qualified scientists – under the guise of national security. Until recently science was the one forum which functioned like an anarchist's dream. Each man capable of doing research had more or less the same opportunity of access to its tools and to a hearing by the community of peers. Now bureaucratization and organization have placed much of science beyond public reach. Indeed, what used to be an international network of scientific information has been splintered into an arena of competing teams. The members as well as the artifacts of the scientific community have been locked into national and corporate programmes oriented towards practical achievement, to the radical impoverishment of the men who support these nations and corporations.

In a world which is controlled and owned by nations and corporations, only limited access to educational objects will ever be possible. But increased access to those objects which can be shared for educational purposes may enlighten us enough to help us to break through these ultimate political barriers. Public schools transfer control over the educational uses of objects from private to professional hands. The institutional inversion of schools could empower the individual to reclaim the right to use them for education. A truly public kind of ownership might begin to emerge if private or corporate control over the educational aspect of 'things' were brought to the vanishing point.

Skill exchanges

A guitar teacher, unlike a guitar, can be neither classified in a museum nor owned by the public nor rented from an educational warehouse. Teachers of skills belong to a different class of resources from objects needed to learn a skill. This is not to say that they are indispensable in every case. I can rent not only a guitar but also taped guitar lessons and illustrated chord charts, and with these things I can teach myself to play the guitar. Indeed, this arrangement may have advantages – if the available tapes are better than the available teachers, or if the only time I have for learning the guitar is late at night, or if the tunes I wish to play are unknown in my country, or if I am shy and prefer to fumble along in privacy.

Skill teachers must be listed and contacted through a different kind of channel from that of things. A thing is available at the bidding of the user – or could be – whereas a person formally becomes a skill resource only when he consents to do so, and he can also restrict time, place and method as he chooses.

Skill teachers must be also distinguished from peers from whom one would learn. Peers who wish to pursue a common inquiry must start from common interests and abilities; they get together to exercise or improve a skill they share: basketball, dancing, constructing a camp site or discussing the next election. The first transmission of a skill, on the other hand, involves bringing together someone who has the skill and someone who does not have it and wants to acquire it.

A 'skill model' is a person who possesses a skill and is willing to demonstrate its practice. A demonstration of this kind is frequently a necessary resource for a potential learner. Modern inventions permit us to incorporate demonstration into tape, film, or chart; yet one would hope personal demonstration will remain in wide demand, especially in communication skills. Some ten thousand adults have learned Spanish at our Center at Cuernavaca – mostly highly motivated persons who wanted to acquire near-native fluency in a second language. When they are faced with a choice between carefully programmed instruction in a lab or drill sessions with two other students and a native speaker following a rigid routine, most choose the second.

For most widely shared skills, a person who demonstrates the skill is the only human resource we ever need or get. Whether in speaking or driving, in cooking or in the use of communication equipment, we are often barely conscious of formal instruction and learning, especially after our first experience of the materials in question. I see no reason why other complex skills, such as the mechanical aspects of surgery and playing the fiddle, of reading or the use of directories and catalogues, could not be learned in the same way.

A well-motivated student who does not labour under a specific handicap often needs no further human assistance than can be provided by someone who can demonstrate on demand how to do what the learner wants to learn to do. The demand made of skilled people that before demonstrating their skill they be certified as pedagogues is a result of the insistence either that people learn what they do not want to know or that all people – even those with a special handicap – learn certain things, at a given moment in their lives, and preferably under specified circumstances.

What makes skills scarce on the present educational market is the institutional requirement that those who can demonstrate them may not do so unless they are given public trust, through a certificate. We insist that those who help others acquire a skill should also know how to diagnose learning difficulties and be able to motivate people to aspire to learn skills. In short, we demand that they be pedagogues. People who can demonstrate skills will be plentiful as soon as we learn to recognize them outside the teaching profession.

Where princelings are being taught, the parents' insistence that the teacher and the person with skills be combined in one person is understandable, if no longer defensible. But for all parents to aspire to have Aristotle for their Alexander is obviously self-defeating. The person who can both inspire students and demonstrate a technique is so rare, and so hard to recognize, that even princelings more often get a sophist than a true philosopher.

A demand for scarce skills can be quickly filled even if there are only small numbers of people to demonstrate them; but such people must be easily available. During the 1940s radio repairmen, most of them with no schooling in their work, were no more than two years behind radios in penetrating the interior of Latin America. There they stayed until transistor radios, which are cheap to purchase and impossible to repair, put them out of business. Technical schools now fail to accomplish what repairmen of equally useful, more durable radios could do as a matter of course.

Converging self-interests now conspire to stop a man from sharing his skill. The man who has the skill profits from its scarcity and not from its reproduction. The teacher who specializes in transmitting the skill profits from the artisan's unwillingness to launch his own apprentice into the field. The public is indoctrinated to believe that skills are valuable and reliable only if they are the result of formal schooling. The job market depends on making skills scarce and on keeping them scarce, either by proscribing their unauthorized use and transmission or by making things which can be operated and repaired only by those who have access to tools or information which are kept scarce.

Schools thus produce shortages of skilled persons. A good example is the diminishing number of nurses in the United States, owing to the rapid increase of four-year B.S. programmes in nursing. Women from poorer families, who would formerly have enrolled in a two- or three-year programme, now stay out of the nursing profession altogether.

Insisting on the certification of teachers is another way of keeping skills scarce. If nurses were encouraged to train nurses, and if nurses were employed on the basis of their proven skill at giving injections, filling in charts and giving medicine, there would soon be no lack of trained nurses. Certification now tends to abridge the freedom of education by converting the civil right to share one's knowledge into the privilege of academic freedom, now conferred only on the employees of a school. To guarantee access to an effective exchange of skills, we need legislation which generalizes academic freedom. The right to teach any skill should come under the protection of freedom of speech. Once restrictions on teaching are removed, they will quickly be removed from learning as well.

The teacher of skills needs some inducement to grant his services to a pupil. There are at least two simple ways to begin to channel public funds to non-certified teachers. One way would be to institutionalize the skill exchange by creating free skill-centres open to the public. Such centres could and should be established in industrialized areas, at least for those skills which are fundamental prerequisites for entering certain apprenticeships – such skills as reading, typing, keeping accounts, foreign languages, computer programming and number manipulation, reading special languages such as that of electrical circuits, manipulation of certain machinery, etc. Another approach would be to give certain groups within the population educational currency good for attendance at skill centres where other clients would have to pay commercial rates.

A much more radical approach would be to create a 'bank' for skill exchange. Each citizen would be given a basic credit with which to acquire fundamental skills. Beyond that minimum, further credits would go to those who earned them by teaching, whether they served as models in organized skill centres or did so privately at home or on the playground. Only those who had taught others for an equivalent amount of time would have a claim on the time of more advanced teachers. An entirely new elite would be promoted, an elite of those who earned their education by sharing it.

Should parents have the right to earn skill credit for their children? Since such an arrangement would give further advantage to the privileged classes, it might be offset by granting a larger credit to the underprivileged. The operation of a skill exchange would depend on the existence of agencies which would facilitate the development of directory information and assure its free and inexpensive use. Such an agency might also provide supplementary services of testing and certification and might help to enforce the legislation required to break up and prevent monopolistic practices.

Fundamentally, the freedom of a universal skill exchange must be guaranteed by laws which permit discrimination only on the basis of tested skills and not on the basis of educational pedigree. Such a guarantee inevitably requires public control over tests which may be used to qualify persons for the job market. Otherwise, it would be possible to surreptitiously re-introduce complex batteries of tests at the work place itself which would serve for social selection. Much could be done to make skill-testing objective, e.g. allowing only the operation of specific machines or systems to be tested. Tests of typing (measured according to speed, number of errors, and whether or not the typist can work from dictation), operation of an ac-counting system or of a hydraulic crane, driving, coding into COBOL, etc., can easily be made objective.

In fact, many of the true skills which are of practical impor-tance can be so tested. And for the purposes of manpower man-agement a test of a current skill level is much more useful than the information that twenty years ago a person satisfied his teacher in a curriculum in which typing, shorthand and ac-counting were taught. The very need for official skill-testing can, of course, be questioned: I personally believe that freedom from undue hurt to a man's reputation through labelling is better guaranteed by restricting than by forbidding tests of com-petence.

Peer-matching

At their worst, schools gather classmates into the same room and subject them to the same sequence of treatment in maths, citi-zenship and spelling. At their best, they permit each student to choose one of a limited number of courses. In any case, groups of peers form around the goals of teachers. A desirable educa-tional system would let each person specify the activity for which he sought a peer.

School does offer children an opportunity to escape their

homes and meet new friends. But, at the same time, this process indoctrinates children with the idea that they should select their friends from among those with whom they are put together. Providing the young from their earliest age with invitations to meet, evaluate and seek out others would prepare them for a lifelong interest in seeking new partners for new endeavours.

A good chess player is always glad to find a close match, and one novice to find another. Clubs serve their purpose. People who want to discuss specific books or articles would probably pay to find discussion partners. People who want to play games, go on excursions, build fish tanks or motorize bicycles will go to considerable lengths to find peers. The reward for their efforts is finding those peers. Good schools try to bring out the common interests of their students registered in the same programme. The inverse of school would be an institution which increased the chances that persons who at a given moment shared the same specific interest could meet — no matter what else they had in common.

Skill-teaching does not provide equal benefits for both parties, as does the matching of peers. The teacher of skills, as I have pointed out, must usually be offered some incentive beyond the rewards of teaching. Skill-teaching is a matter of repeating drills over and over and is, in fact, all the more dreary for those pupils who need it most. A skill exchange needs currency or credits or other tangible incentives in order to operate, even if the exchange itself were to generate a currency of its own. A peer-matching system requires no such incentives, but only a communications network.

Tapes, retrieval systems, programmed instruction and reproduction of shapes and sounds tend to reduce the need for recourse to human teachers of many skills; they increase the efficiency of teachers and the number of skills one can pick up in a lifetime. Parallel to this runs an increased need to meet people interested in enjoying the newly acquired skill. A student who has picked up Greek before her vacation would like to discuss in Greek Cretan politics when she returns. A Mexican in New York wants to find other readers of the paper *Siempre* — or of '*Los Agachados*', the most popular comic book. Somebody else wants to meet peers who, like himself, would like to increase their interest in the work of James Baldwin or of Bolívar.

The operation of a peer-matching network would be simple. The user would identify himself by name and address and describe the activity for which he sought a peer. A computer would send him back the names and addresses of all those who had inserted the same description. It is amazing that such a simple utility has never been used on a broad scale for publicly valued activity.

In its most rudimentary form, communication between client and computer could be established by return mail. In big cities typewriter terminals could provide instantaneous responses. The only way to retrieve a name and address from the computer would be to list an activity for which a peer was sought. People using the system would become known only to their potential peers.

A complement to the computer could be a network of bulletin boards and classified newspaper ads, listing the activities for which the computer could not produce a match. No names would have to be given. Interested readers would then introduce their names into the system. A publicly supported peer-match network might be the only way to guarantee the right of free assembly and to train people in the exercise of this most fundamental civic activity.

The right of free assembly has been politically recognized and culturally accepted. We should now understand that this right is curtailed by laws that make some forms of assembly obligatory. This is especially the case with institutions which conscript according to age group, class or sex, and which are very time-consuming. The army is one example. School is an even more outrageous one.

To deschool means to abolish the power of one person to oblige another person to attend a meeting. It also means recognizing the right of any person, of any age or sex, to call a meeting. This right has been drastically diminished by the institutionalization of meetings. 'Meeting' originally referred to the result of an individual's act of gathering. Now it refers to the institutional product of some agency.

The ability of service institutions to acquire clients has far outgrown the ability of individuals to be heard independently of institutional media, which respond to individuals only if they are saleable news. Peer-matching facilities should be available for individuals who want to bring people together as easily as the village bell called the villagers to council. School buildings – of doubtful value for conversion to other uses – could often serve this purpose.

The school system, in fact, may soon face a problem which churches have faced before: what to do with surplus space emptied by the defection of the faithful. Schools are as difficult to sell as temples. One way to provide for their continued use would be to give over the space to people from the neighbourhood. Each could state what he would do in the classroom and when, and a bulletin board would bring the available programmes to the attention of the inquirers. Access to 'class' would be free – or purchased with educational vouchers. The 'teacher' could even be paid according to the number of pupils he could attract for any full two-hour period. I can imagine that very young leaders and great educators would be the two types most prominent in such a system. The same approach could be taken towards higher education. Students could be furnished with educational vouchers which entitled them to ten hours' yearly private consultation with the teacher of their choice – and, for the rest of their learning, depend on the library, the peer-matching network and apprenticeships.

We must, of course, recognize the probability that such public matching devices would be abused for exploitative and immoral purposes, just as the telephone and the mails have been so abused. As with those networks, there must be some protection. I have proposed elsewhere a matching system which would allow only pertinent printed information, plus the name and address of the inquirer, to be used. Such a system would be virtually foolproof against abuse. Other arrangements could allow the addition of any book, film, TV programme or other item quoted from a special catalogue. Concern about the dangers of the system should not make us lose sight of its far greater benefits.

Some who share my concern for free speech and assembly will argue that peer-matching is an artificial means of bringing people together and would not be used by the poor – who need it most. Some people become genuinely agitated when one suggests the setting up of ad hoc encounters which are not rooted in the life of a local community. Others react when one suggests using a computer to sort and match client-identified interests. People cannot be drawn together in such an impersonal manner, they say. Common inquiry must be rooted in a history of shared experience at many levels, and must grow out of this experience – the development of neighbourhood institutions, for example.

I sympathize with these objections, but I think they miss my point as well as their own. In the first place, the return to neighbourhood life as the primary centre of creative expression might actually work against the re-establishment of neighbourhoods as political units. Centring demands on the neighbourhood may, in fact, neglect an important liberating aspect of urban life – the ability of a person to participate simultaneously in several peer groups. Also, there is an important sense in which people who have never lived together in a physical community may occasionally have far more experiences to share than those who have known each other from childhood. The great religions have always recognized the importance of far-off encounters, and the faithful have always found freedom through them; pilgrimage, monasticism, the mutual support of temples and sanctuaries reflect this awareness. Peer-matching could significantly help in making explicit the many potential but suppressed communities of the city.

Local communities are valuable. They are also a vanishing reality as men progressively let service institutions define their circles of social relationship. Milton Kotler in his recent book has shown that the imperialism of 'downtown' deprives the neighbourhood of its political significance. The protectionist attempt to resurrect the neighbourhood as a cultural unit only supports this bureaucratic imperialism. Far from artificially removing men from their local contexts to join abstract groupings, peer-matching should encourage the restoration of local life to cities from which it is now disappearing. A man who recovers his initiative to call his fellows into meaningful conversation may cease to settle for being separated from them by office protocol or suburban etiquette. Having once seen that doing things together depends on deciding to do so, men may even insist that their local communities become more open to creative political exchange.

We must recognize that city life tends to become immensely costly as city-dwellers must be taught to rely for every one of their needs on complex institutional services. It is extremely expensive to keep it even minimally liveable. Peer-matching in the city could be a first step towards breaking down the dependence of citizens on bureaucratic civic services.

It would also be an essential step to providing new means of establishing public trust. In a schooled society we have come to rely more and more on the professional judgement of educators on the effect of their own work in order to decide whom we can or cannot trust: we go to the doctor, lawyer or psychologist because we trust that anybody with the required amount of specialized educational treatment by other colleagues deserves our confidence.

In a deschooled society professionals could no longer claim the trust of their clients on the basis of their curricular pedigree, or ensure their standing by simply referring their clients to other professionals who approved of their schooling. Instead of placing trust in professionals, it should be possible, at any time, for any potential client to consult with other experienced clients of a professional about their satisfaction with him by means of another peer network easily set up by computer, or by a number of other means. Such networks could be seen as public utilities which permitted students to choose their teachers or patients their healers.

Professional educators

As citizens have new choices, new chances for learning, their willingness to seek leadership should increase. We may expect that they will experience more deeply both their own independence and their need for guidance. As they are liberated from manipulation by others, they should learn to profit from the discipline others have acquired in a lifetime. Deschooling education should increase – rather than stifle – the search for men with practical wisdom who would be willing to sustain the newcomer in his educational adventure. As masters of their art abandon the claim to be superior informants or skill models, their claim to superior wisdom will begin to ring true.

With an increasing demand for masters, their supply should also increase. As the schoolmaster vanishes, conditions will arise which should bring forth the vocation of the independent educator. This may seem almost a contradiction in terms, so thoroughly have schools and teachers become complementary. Yet this is exactly what the development of the first three educational exchanges would tend to result in – and what would be required to permit their full exploitation – for parents and other 'natural educators' need guidance, individual learners need assistance, and the networks need people to operate them.

Parents need guidance in directing their children on the road that leads to responsible educational independence. Learners need experienced leadership when they encounter rough terrain. These two needs are quite distinct: the first is a need for pedagogy, the second for intellectual leadership in all other fields of knowledge. The first calls for knowledge of human learning and of educational resources, the second for wisdom based on experience in any kind of exploration. Both kinds of experience are indispensable for effective educational endeavour. Schools package these functions into one role – and render the independent exercise of any of them if not disreputable at least suspect.

Three types of special educational competence should, in fact, be distinguished: one to create and operate the kinds of educational exchanges or networks outlined here; another to guide students and parents in the use of these networks; and a third to act as *primus inter pares* in undertaking difficult intellectual exploratory journeys. Only the former two can be conceived of as branches of an independent profession: educational administrators and pedagogical counsellors. To design and operate the networks I have been describing would not require many people, but it would require people with the most profound understanding of education and administration, in a perspective quite different from and even opposed to that of schools.

While an independent educational profession of this kind

would welcome many people whom the schools exclude, it would also exclude many whom the schools qualify. The establishment and operation of educational networks would require some designers and administrators, but not in the numbers or of the type required by the administration of schools. Student discipline, public relations, hiring, supervising and firing teachers would have neither place nor counterpart in the networks I have been describing. Neither would curriculum-making, textbook-purchasing, the maintenance of grounds and facilities, or the supervision of interscholastic athletic competition. Nor would child custody, lesson-planning and record-keeping, which now take up so much of the time of teachers, figure in the operation of educational networks. Instead, the operation of learning webs would require some of the skills and attitudes now expected from the staff of a museum, a library, an executive employment agency or a *maître d'hôtel*.

Today's educational administrators are concerned with controlling teachers and students to the satisfaction of others – trustees, legislatures and corporate executives. Network builders and administrators would have to demonstrate genius at keeping themselves, and others, out of people's way, at facilitating encounters among students, skill models, educational leaders and educational objects. Many persons now attracted to teaching are profoundly authoritarian and would not be able to assume this task: building educational exchanges would mean making it easy for people – especially the young – to pursue goals which might contradict the ideals of the traffic manager who makes the pursuit possible.

If the networks I have described could emerge, the educational path of each student would be his own to follow, and only in retrospect would it take on the features of a recognizable programme. The wise student would periodically seek professional advice: assistance to set a new goal, insight into difficulties encountered, choice between possible methods. Even now, most persons would admit that the important services their teachers have rendered them are such advice or counsel, given at a chance meeting or in a tutorial. Pedagogues, in an unschooled world, would also come into their own, and be able to do what frustrated teachers pretend to pursue today.

While network administrators would concentrate primarily on the building and maintenance of roads providing access to resources, the pedagogue would help the student to find the path which for him could lead fastest to his goal. If a student wanted to learn spoken Cantonese from a Chinese neighbour, the pedagogue would be available to judge their proficiency, and to help them select the textbook and methods most suitable to their talents, character and the time available for study. He could counsel the would-be aeroplane mechanic on finding the best places for apprenticeship. He could recommend books to somebody who wanted to find challenging peers to discuss African history. Like the network administrator, the pedagogical counsellor would conceive of himself as a professional educator. Access to either could be gained by individuals through the use of educational vouchers.

The role of the educational initiator or leader, the master or 'true' leader, is somewhat more elusive than that of the professional administrator or the pedagogue. This is so because leadership is itself hard to define. In practice, an individual is a leader if people follow his initiative and become apprentices in his progressive discoveries. Frequently, this involves a prophetic vision of entirely new standards – quite understandable today – in which present 'wrong' will turn out to be 'right'. In a society which would honour the right to call assemblies through peer-matching, the ability to take educational initiative on a specific subject would be as wide as access to learning itself. But, of course, there is a vast difference between the initiative taken by someone to call a fruitful meeting to discuss this essay and the ability of someone to provide leadership in the systematic exploration of its implications.

Leadership also does not depend on being right. As Thomas Kuhn points out, in a period of constantly changing paradigms most of the very distinguished leaders are bound to be proven wrong by the test of hindsight. Intellectual leadership does depend on superior intellectual discipline and imagination and the willingness to associate with others in their exercise. A learner, for example, may think that there is an analogy between the US anti-slavery movement or the Cuban Revolution and what is happening in Harlem. The educator who is himself a historian can show him how to appreciate the flaws in such an analogy. He may retrace his own steps as a historian. He may invite the learner to participate in his own research. In both cases he will apprentice his pupil in a critical art – which is rare in school – and which money or other favours cannot buy.

The relationship of master and disciple is not restricted to intellectual discipline. It has its counterpart in the arts, in physics, in religion, in psychoanalysis and in pedagogy. It fits mountain-climbing, silver-working and politics, cabinet-making and personnel administration. What is common to all true master–pupil relationships is the awareness both share that their relationship is literally priceless and in very different ways a privilege for both.

Charlatans, demagogues, proselytizers, corrupt masters and simoniacal priests, tricksters, miracle workers and messiahs have proven capable of assuming leadership roles and thus show the dangers of any dependence of a disciple on the master. Different societies have taken different measures to defend themselves against these counterfeit teachers. Indians relied on caste-lineage, Eastern Jews on the spiritual discipleship of rabbis, high periods of Christianity on an exemplary life of monastic virtue, other periods on hierarchical orders. Our society relies on certification by schools. It is doubtful that this procedure provides a better screening, but if it should be claimed that it does, then the counter-claim can be made that it does so at the cost of making personal discipleship almost vanish.

In practice, there will always be a fuzzy line between the teacher of skills and the educational leaders identified above, and there are no practical reasons why access to some leaders could not be gained by discovering the 'master' in the drill teacher who introduces students to his discipline.

On the other hand, what characterizes the true master-disciple relationship is its priceless character. Aristotle speaks of it as a 'moral type of friendship, which is not on fixed terms: it makes a gift, or does whatever it does, as to a friend'. Thomas Aquinas says of this kind of teaching that inevitably it is an act of love and mercy. This kind of teaching is always a luxury for the teacher and a form of leisure (in Greek, 'schole') for him and his pupil: an activity meaningful for both, having no ulterior purpose.

To rely for true intellectual leadership on the desire of gifted people to provide it is obviously necessary even in our society, but it could not be made into a policy now. We must first construct a society in which personal acts themselves reacquire a value higher than that of making things and manipulating people. In such a society exploratory, inventive, creative teaching would logically be counted among the most desirable forms of leisurely 'unemployment'. But we do not have to wait until the advent of utopia. Even now one of the most important consequences of deschooling and the establishment of peer-matching facilities would be the initiative which 'masters' could take to assemble congenial disciples. It would also, as we have seen, provide ample opportunity for potential disciples to share information or to select a master.

Schools are not the only institutions which pervert professions by packaging roles. Hospitals render home care increasingly impossible – and then justify hospitalization as a benefit to the sick. At the same time, the doctor's legitimacy and ability to work come increasingly to depend on his association with a hospital, even though he is still less totally dependent on it than are teachers on schools. The same could be said about courts, which overcrowd their calendars as new transactions acquire legal solemnity, and thus delay justice. Or it could be said about churches, which succeed in making a captive profession out of a free vocation. The result in each case is scarce service at higher cost, and greater income to the less competent members of the profession.

So long as the older professions monopolize superior income and prestige it is difficult to reform them. The profession of the schoolteacher should be easier to reform, and not only because it is of more recent origin. The educational profession now claims a comprehensive monopoly; it claims the exclusive competence to apprentice not only its own novices but those of other professions as well. This over-expansion renders it vulnerable to any profession which would reclaim the right to teach its own apprentices. Schoolteachers are overwhelmingly badly paid and frustrated by the tight control of the school system. The most enterprising and gifted among them would probably find more congenial work, more independence and even higher incomes by specializing as skill models, network administrators or guidance specialists.

Finally, the dependence of the registered student on the certified teacher can be broken more easily than his dependence on other professionals – for instance, that of a hospitalized patient on his doctor. If schools ceased to be compulsory, teachers who find their satisfaction in the exercise of pedagogical authority in the classroom would be left only with pupils who were attracted by their style. The disestablishment of our present professional structure could begin with the dropping out of the schoolteacher.

The disestablishment of schools will inevitably happen – and it will happen surprisingly fast. It cannot be retarded very much longer, and it is hardly necessary to promote it vigorously, for this is being done now. What is worthwhile is to try to orient it in a hopeful direction, for it could take place in either of two diametrically opposed ways.

The first would be the expansion of the mandate of the pedagogue and his increasing control over society even outside school. With the best of intentions and simply by expanding the rhetoric now used in school, the present crisis in the schools could provide educators with an excuse to use all the networks of contemporary society to funnel their messages to us – for our own good. Deschooling, which we cannot stop, could mean the advent of a 'brave new world' dominated by well-intentioned administrators of programmed instruction.

On the other hand, the growing awareness on the part of governments, as well as of employers, taxpayers, enlightened pedagogues and school administrators, that graded curricular teaching for certification has become harmful could offer large masses of people an extraordinary opportunity: that of preserving the right of equal access to the tools both of learning and of sharing with others what they know or believe. But this would require that the educational revolution be guided by certain goals:

1. To liberate access to things by abolishing the control which persons and institutions now exercise over their educational values.

2. To liberate the sharing of skills by guaranteeing freedom to teach or exercise them on request.

3. To liberate the critical and creative resources of people by returning to individual persons the ability to call and hold meetings – an ability now increasingly monopolized by institutions which claim to speak for the people.

4. To liberate the individual from the obligation to shape his expectations to the services offered by an established profession – by providing him with the opportunity to draw on the experience of his peers and to entrust himself to the teacher, guide, adviser or healer of his choice. Inevitably the deschooling of society will blur the distinctions between economics, education and politics on which the stability of the present world order and the stability of nations now rest.

Our review of educational institutions leads us to a review of our image of man. The creature whom schools need as a client has neither the autonomy nor the motivation to grow on his own. We can recognize universal schooling as the culmination of a Promethean enterprise, and speak about the alternative as a world fit to live in for Epimethean man. While we can specify that the alternative to scholastic funnels is a world made transparent by true communication webs, and while we can specify very concretely how these could function, we can only expect the Epimethean nature of man to re-emerge; we can neither plan nor produce it.

7 Rebirth of Epimethean Man

Our society resembles the ultimate machine which I once saw in a New York toy shop. It was a metal casket which, when you touched a switch, snapped open to reveal a mechanical hand. Chromed fingers reached out for the lid, pulled it down and locked it from the inside. It was a box; you expected to be able to take something out of it; yet all it contained was a mechanism for closing the cover. This contraption is the opposite of Pandora's 'box'.

The original Pandora, the All-Giver, was an Earth goddess in prehistoric matriarchal Greece. She let all ills escape from her amphora (*pythos*). But she closed the lid before Hope could escape. The history of modern man begins with the degradation of Pandora's myth and comes to an end in the self-sealing casket. It is the history of the Promethean endeavour to forge institutions in order to corral each of the rampant ills. It is the history of fading hope and rising expectations.

To understand what this means we must rediscover the distinction between hope and expectation. Hope, in its strong sense, means trusting faith in the goodness of nature, while expectation, as I will use it here, means reliance on results which are planned and controlled by man. Hope centres desire on a person from whom we await a gift. Expectation looks forward to satisfaction from a predictable process which will produce what we have the right to claim. The Promethean ethos has now eclipsed hope. Survival of the human race depends on its rediscovery as a social force.

The original Pandora was sent to Earth with a jar which contained all ills; of good things, it contained only hope. Primitive man lived in this world of hope. He relied on the munificence of nature, on the handouts of gods, and on the instincts of his tribe to enable him to subsist. Classical Greeks began to replace

hope with expectations. In their version of Pandora she re-
leased both evils and goods. They remembered her mainly for
the ills she had unleashed. And, most significantly, they forgot
that the All-Giver was also the keeper of hope

The Greeks told the story of two brothers, Prometheus and
Epimetheus. The former warned the latter to leave Pandora
alone. Instead, he married her. In classical Greece the name
'Epimetheus', which means 'hindsight', was interpreted to
mean 'dull' or 'dumb'. By the time Hesiod retold the story in
its classical form, the Greeks had become moral and misogyn-
ous patriarchs who panicked at the thought of the first woman.
They built a rational and authoritarian society. Men engineered
institutions through which they planned to cope with the rampant ills. They became conscious of their power to fashion the
world and make it produce services they also learned to expect.
They wanted their own needs and the future demands of their
children to be shaped by their artifacts. They became lawgivers,
architects and authors, the makers of constitutions, cities and
works of art to serve as examples for their offspring. Primitive
man had relied on mythical participation in sacred rites to initiate individuals into the lore of society, but the classical Greeks
recognized as true men only those citizens who let themselves
be fitted by *paideia* (education) into the institutions their elders
had planned.

The developing myth reflects the transition from a world in
which dreams were *interpreted* to a world in which oracles were
made. From immemorial time, the Earth Goddess had been
worshipped on the slope of Mount Parnassus, which was the
centre and navel of the Earth. There, at Delphi (from *delphys*,
the womb), slept Gaia, the sister of Chaos and Eros. Her son,
Python the dragon, guarded her moonlit and dewy dreams, until Apollo the Sun God, the architect of Troy, rose from the
east, slew the dragon, and became the owner of Gaia's cave. His
priests took over her temple. They employed a local maiden, sat
her on a tripod over Earth's smoking navel, and made her
drowsy with fumes. They then rhymed her ecstatic utterances
into hexameters of self-fulfilling prophecies. From all over the
Peloponnesus men brought their problems to Apollo's sanctu-
ary. The oracle was consulted on social options, such as

measures to be taken to stop a plague or a famine, to choose the right constitution for Sparta or the propitious sites for cities which later became Byzantium and Chalcedon. The never-erring arrow became Apollo's symbol. Everything about him became purposeful and useful.

In the *Republic*, describing the ideal state, Plato already excludes popular music. Only the harp and Apollo's lyre would be permitted in towns because their harmony alone creates 'the strain of necessity and the strain of freedom, the strain of the unfortunate and the strain of the fortunate, the strain of courage and the strain of temperance which befit the citizen'. City-dwellers panicked before Pan's flute and its power to awaken the instincts. Only 'the shepherds may play [Pan's] pipes and they only in the country'.

Man assumed responsibility for the laws under which he wanted to live and for the casting of the environment into his own image. Primitive initiation by Mother Earth into mythical life was transformed into the education (*paideia*) of the citizen who would feel at home in the forum.

To the primitive the world was governed by fate, fact and necessity. By stealing fire from the gods, Prometheus turned facts into problems, called necessity into question and defied fate. Classical man framed a civilized context for human perspective. He was aware that he could defy fate–nature–environment, but only at his own risk. Contemporary man goes further; he attempts to create the world in his image, to build a totally man-made environment, and then discovers that he can do so only on the condition of constantly remaking himself to fit it. We now must face the fact that man himself is at stake.

Life today in New York produces a very peculiar vision of what is and what can be, and without this vision life in New York is impossible. A child on the streets of New York never touches anything which has not been scientifically developed, engineered, planned and sold to someone. Even the trees are there because the Parks Department decided to put them there. The jokes the child hears on television have been programmed at a high cost. The refuse with which he plays in the streets of Harlem is made of broken packages planned for somebody else. Even desires and fears are institutionally shaped. Power and violence are organized and managed: the gangs versus the police. Learning itself is defined as the consumption of subject matter, which is the result of researched, planned and promoted programmes. Whatever good there is, is the product of some specialized institution. It would be foolish to demand something which some institution cannot produce. The child of the city cannot expect anything which lies outside the possible development of institutional process. Even his fantasy is prompted to produce science fiction. He can experience the poetic surprise of the unplanned only through his encounter with 'dirt', blunder or failure: the orange peel in the gutter, the puddle in the street, the breakdown of order, programme, or machine are the only take-offs for creative fancy. 'Goofing off' becomes the only poetry at hand.

Since there is nothing desirable which has not been planned, the city child soon concludes that we will always be able to design an institution for our every want. He takes for granted the power of process to create value. Whether the goal is meeting a mate, integrating a neighbourhood or acquiring reading skills, it will be defined in such a way that its achievement can be engineered. The man who knows that nothing in demand is out of production soon expects that nothing produced can be out of demand. If a moon vehicle can be designed, so can the demand to go to the moon. Not to go where one can go would be subversive. It would unmask as folly the assumption that every satisfied demand entails the discovery of an even greater unsatisfied one. Such insight would stop progress. Not to produce what is possible would expose the law of 'rising expectations' as a euphemism for a growing frustration gap, which is the motor of a society built on the coproduction of services and increased demand.

The state of mind of the modern city-dweller appears in the mythical tradition only under the image of Hell: Sisyphus, who for a while had chained Thanatos (death), must roll a heavy stone up the hill to the pinnacle of Hell, and the stone always slips from his grip just when he is about to reach the top. Tantalus, who was invited by the gods to share their meal, and on that occasion stole their secret of how to prepare all-healing ambrosia, which bestowed immortality, suffers eternal hunger and thirst standing in a river of receding waters, overshadowed by fruit trees with receding branches. A world of ever-rising demands is not just evil – it can be spoken of only as Hell.

Man has developed the frustrating power to demand anything because he cannot visualize anything which an institution cannot do for him. Surrounded by all-powerful tools, man is reduced to a tool of his tools. Each of the institutions meant to exorcise one of the primeval evils has become a fail-safe, self-sealing coffin for man. Man is trapped in the boxes he makes to contain the ills Pandora allowed to escape. The blackout of reality in the smog produced by our tools has enveloped us. Quite suddenly we find ourselves in the darkness of our own trap.

Reality itself has become dependent on human decision. The same President who ordered the ineffective invasion of Cambodia could equally well order the effective use of the atom. The 'Hiroshima switch' now can cut the navel of the Earth. Man has acquired the power to make Chaos overwhelm both Eros and Gaia. This new power of man to cut the navel of the Earth is a constant reminder that our institutions not only create their own ends, but also have the power to put an end to themselves and to us. The absurdity of modern institutions is evident in the case of the military. Modern weapons can defend freedom, civilization, and life only by annihilating them. Security in military language means the ability to do away with the Earth.

The absurdity that underlies non-military institutions is no less manifest. There is no switch in them to activate their destructive power, but neither do they need a switch. Their grip is already fastened to the lid of the world. They create needs faster than they can create satisfaction, and in the process of trying to meet the needs they generate, they consume the Earth. This is true for agriculture and manufacturing, and no less for medicine and education. Modern agriculture poisons and exhausts the soil. The 'green revolution' can, by means of new seeds, triple the output of an acre – but only with an even greater proportional increase of fertilizers, insecticides, water and power. Manufacturing of these, as of all other goods, pollutes the oceans and the atmosphere and degrades irreplaceable resources. If combustion continues to increase at present rates, we will soon consume the oxygen of the atmosphere faster than it can be replaced. We have no reason to believe that fission or fusion can replace combustion without equal or higher hazards. Medicine men replace midwives and promise to make man into something else: genetically planned, pharmacologically sweetened and capable of more protracted sickness. The contemporary ideal is a pan-hygienic world: a world in which all contacts between men, and between men and their world, are the result of foresight and manipulation. School has become the planned process which tools man for a planned world, the principal tool to trap man in man's trap. It is supposed to shape each man to an adequate level for playing a part in this world game. Inexorably we cultivate, treat, produce and school the world out of existence.

The military institution is evidently absurd. The absurdity of non-military institutions is more difficult to face. It is even more frightening, precisely because it operates inexorably. We know which switch must stay open to avoid an atomic holocaust. No switch detains an ecological Armageddon.

In classical antiquity, man had discovered that the world could be made according to man's plans, and with this insight he perceived that it was inherently precarious, dramatic and comical. Democratic institutions evolved and man was presumed worthy of trust within their framework. Expectations from due process and confidence in human nature kept each other in balance. The traditional professions developed and with them the institutions needed for their exercise.

Surreptitiously, reliance on institutional process has replaced dependence on personal good will. The world has lost its humane dimension and reacquired the factual necessity and fatefulness which were characteristic of primitive times. But while the chaos of the barbarian was constantly ordered in the name of mysterious, anthropomorphic gods, today only man's planning can be given as a reason for the world being as it is. Man has become the plaything of scientists, engineers and planners.

We see this logic at work in our selves and in others. I know a Mexican village through which not more than a dozen cars drive each day. A Mexican was playing dominoes on the new hard-surface road in front of his house – where he had probably played and sat since his youth. A car sped through and killed him. The tourist who reported the event to me was deeply upset, and yet he said: 'The man had it coming to him.'

At first sight, the tourist's remark is no different from the statement of some primitive Bushman reporting the death of a fellow who had collided with a taboo and had therefore died. But the two statements carry opposite meanings. The primitive can blame some tremendous and dumb transcendence, while the tourist is in awe of the inexorable logic of the machine. The primitive does not sense responsibility; the tourist senses it, but denies it. In both the primitive and the tourist the classical mode of drama, the style of tragedy, the logic of personal endeavour and rebellion is absent. The primitive man has not become conscious of it, and the tourist has lost it. The myth of the Bushman and the myth of the American are made of inert, inhuman forces. Neither experiences tragic rebellion. For the Bushman, the event follows the laws of magic; for the American, it follows the laws of science. The event puts him under the spell of the laws of mechanics, which for him govern physical, social and psychological events.

The mood of 1971 is propitious for a major change of direction in search of a hopeful future. Institutional goals continuously contradict institutional products. The poverty programme produces more poor, the war in Asia more Vietcong, technical assistance more underdevelopment. Birth-control clinics increase survival rates and boost the population; schools produce more dropouts; and the curb on one kind of pollution usually increases another.

Consumers are faced with the realization that the more they can buy, the more deceptions they must swallow. Until recently it seemed logical that the blame for this pandemic inflation of dysfunctions could be laid either on the limping of scientific discovery behind the technological demands or on the perversity of ethnic, ideological or class enemies. Both the expectations of a scientific millennium and of a war to end all wars have declined.

For the experienced consumer, there is no way back to a naïve reliance on magical technologies. Too many people have had bad experiences with neurotic computers, hospital-bred infections, and jams wherever there is traffic on the road, in the air or on the phone. Only ten years ago conventional wisdom anticipated a better life based on an increase in scientific discovery. Now scientists frighten children. The moon shots provide a fascinating demonstration that human failure can be almost eliminated among the operators of complex systems – yet this does not allay our fears that the human failure to consume according to instruction might spread out of control.

For the social reformer there is no way back, either, to the assumptions of the 1940s. The hope has vanished that the problem of justly distributing goods can be sidetracked by creating an abundance of them. The cost of the minimum packages capable of satisfying modern tastes has skyrocketed, and what makes tastes modern is their obsolescence prior even to satisfaction.

The limits of the Earth's resources have become evident. No breakthrough in science or technology could provide every man in the world with the commodities and services which are now availabe to the poor of rich countries. For instance, it would take the extraction of one hundred times the present amounts of iron, tin, copper and lead to achieve such a goal, with even the 'lightest' alternative technology.

Finally, teachers, doctors and social workers realize that their distinct professional ministrations have one aspect – at least – in common. They create further demands for the institutional treatments they provide, faster than they can provide service institutions.

Not just some part, but the very logic, of conventional wisdom is becoming suspect. Even the laws of economy seem unconvincing outside the narrow parameters which apply to the social, geographic area where most of the money is concentrated. Money is, indeed, the cheapest currency, but only in an economy geared to efficiency measured in monetary terms. Both capitalist and Communist countries in their various forms are committed to measuring efficiency in cost-benefit ratios expressed in dollars. Capitalism flaunts a higher standard of living as its claim to superiority. Communism boasts of a higher growth rate as an index of its ultimate triumph. But under either ideology the total cost of increasing efficiency increases geometrically. The largest institutions compete most fiercely for resources which are not listed in any inventory: the air, the ocean, silence, sunlight and health. They bring the scarcity of these resources to public attention only when they are almost irremediably degraded. Everywhere nature becomes poisonous, society inhumane and the inner life is invaded and personal vocation smothered.

A society committed to the institutionalization of values identifies the production of goods and services with the demand for such. Education which makes you need the product is included in the price of the product. School is the advertising agency which makes you believe that you need the society as it is. In such a society marginal value has become constantly self-transcendent. It forces the few largest consumers to compete for the power to deplete the earth, to fill their own swelling bellies, to discipline smaller consumers, and to deactivate those who still find satisfaction in making do with what they have. The ethos of non-satiety is thus at the root of physical depredation, social polarization and psychological passivity.

When values have been institutionalized in planned and engineered processes, members of modern society believe that the good life consists in having institutions which define the values that both they and their society believe they need. Institutional value can be defined as the level of output of an institution. The corresponding value of man is measured by his ability to consume and degrade these institutional outputs, and thus create a new – even higher – demand. The value of institutionalized man depends on his capacity as an incinerator. To use an image – he has become the idol of his handiworks. Man now defines himself as the furnace which burns up the values produced by his tools. And there is no limit to his capacity. His is the act of Prometheus carried to an extreme.

The exhaustion and pollution of the earth's resources is, above all, the result of a corruption in man's self-image, of a regression in his consciousness. Some would like to speak about a mutation of collective consciousness which leads to a conception of man as an organism dependent not on nature and individuals, but rather on institutions. This institutionalization of substantive values, this belief that a planned process of treat-

ment ultimately gives results desired by the recipient, this consumer ethos, is at the heart of the Promethean fallacy.

Efforts to find a new balance in the global milieu depend on
the deinstitutionalization of values.

The suspicion that something is structurally wrong with the
vision of *homo faber* is common to a growing minority in capitalist, Communist and 'underdeveloped' countries alike. This
suspicion is the shared characteristic of a new elite. To it belong
people of all classes, incomes, faiths and civilizations. They have
become wary of the myths of the majority: of scientific utopias,
of ideological diabolism, and of the expectation of the distribution of goods and services with some degree of equality. They
share with the majority the sense of being trapped. They share
with the majority the awareness that most new policies adopted
by broad consensus consistently lead to results which are glar-
ingly opposed to their stated aims. Yet whereas the Promethean
majority of would-be spacemen still evades the structural issue,
the emergent minority is critical of the scientific *deus ex
machina,* the ideological panacea and the hunt for devils and
witches. This minority begins to formulate its suspicion that
our constant deceptions tie us to contemporary institutions as
the chains bound Prometheus to his rock. Hopeful trust and
classical irony (*eironeia*) must conspire to expose the Promethean fallacy.

Prometheus is usually thought to mean 'foresight', or sometimes even 'he who makes the North Star progress'. He tricked
the gods out of their monopoly of fire, taught men to use it in
the forging of iron, became the god of technologists and wound
up in iron chains.

The Pythia of Delphi has now been replaced by a computer
which hovers above panels and punch cards. The hexameters of
the oracle have given way to sixteen-bit codes of instructions.
Man the helmsman has turned the rudder over to the cyber-
netic machine. The ultimate machine emerges to direct our des-
tinies. Children fantasize flying their spacecrafts away from a
crepuscular earth.

From the perspectives of the Man on the Moon, Prometheus
could recognize sparkling blue Gaia as the planet of Hope and
as the Arc of Mankind. A new sense of the finiteness of the

Earth and a new nostalgia now can open man's eyes to the choice of his brother Epimetheus to wed the Earth with Pandora.

At this point the Greek myth turns into hopeful prophecy because it tells us that the son of Prometheus was Deucalion, the Helmsman of the Ark who like Noah outrode the Flood to become the father of a new mankind which he made from the earth with Pyrrha, the daughter of Epimetheus and Pandora. We are gaining insight into the meaning of the Pythos which Pandora brought from the gods as being the inverse of the Box: our Vessel and Ark.

We now need a name for those who value hope above expectations. We need a name for those who love people more than products, those who believe that

No people are uninteresting,
Their fate is like the chronicle of planets.

Nothing in them is not particular,
and planet is dissimilar from planet.

We need a name for those who love the earth on which each can meet the other,

And if a man lived in obscurity
making his friends in that obscurity,
obscurity is not uninteresting.

We need a name for those who collaborate with their Promethean brother in the lighting of the fire and the shaping of iron, but who do so to enhance their ability to tend and care and wait upon the other, knowing that

to each his world is private,
and in that world one excellent minute.
And in that world one tragic minute.
These are private.*

I suggest that these hopeful brothers and sisters be called Epimethean men.

*The three quotations are from 'People' from the book *Selected Poems* by Yevgeny Yevtushenko, translated and with an Introduction by Robin Milner-Gulland and Peter Levi, published in Penguin Books, 1962.

FOR THE BEST IN PAPERBACKS, LOOK FOR THE

In every corner of the world, on every subject under the sun, Penguin represents quality and variety – the very best in publishing today.

For complete information about books available from Penguin – including Pelicans, Puffins, Peregrines and Penguin Classics – and how to order them, write to us at the appropriate address below. Please note that for copyright reasons the selection of books varies from country to country.

In the United Kingdom: Please write to *Dept E.P., Penguin Books Ltd, Harmondsworth, Middlesex, UB7 0DA*

In the United States: Please write to *Dept BA, Penguin, 299 Murray Hill Parkway, East Rutherford, New Jersey 07073*

In Canada: Please write to *Penguin Books Canada Ltd, 2801 John Street, Markham, Ontario L3R 1B4*

In Australia: Please write to the *Marketing Department, Penguin Books Australia Ltd, P.O. Box 257, Ringwood, Victoria 3134*

In New Zealand: Please write to the *Marketing Department, Penguin Books (NZ) Ltd, Private Bag, Takapuna, Auckland 9*

In India: Please write to *Penguin Overseas Ltd, 706 Eros Apartments, 56 Nehru Place, New Delhi, 110019*

In Holland: Please write to *Penguin Books Nederland B.V., Postbus 195, NL–1380AD Weesp, Netherlands*

In Germany: Please write to *Penguin Books Ltd, Friedrichstrasse 10–12, D–6000 Frankfurt Main 1, Federal Republic of Germany*

In Spain: Please write to *Longman Penguin España, Calle San Nicolas 15, E–28013 Madrid, Spain*

In France: Please write to *Penguin Books Ltd, 39 Rue de Montmorency, F-75003, Paris, France*

In Japan: Please write to *Longman Penguin Japan Co Ltd, Yamaguchi Building, 2–12–9 Kanda Jimbocho, Chiyoda-Ku, Tokyo 101, Japan*

The Second World War (6 volumes) Winston S. Churchill

The definitive history of the cataclysm which swept the world for the second time in thirty years.

1917: The Russian Revolutions and the Origins of Present-Day Communism Leonard Schapiro

A superb narrative history of one of the greatest episodes in modern history by one of our greatest historians.

Imperial Spain 1496–1716 J. H. Elliot

A brilliant modern study of the sudden rise of a barren and isolated country to be the greatest power on earth, and of its equally sudden decline. 'Outstandingly good' – *Daily Telegraph*

Joan of Arc: The Image of Female Heroism Marina Warner

'A profound book, about human history in general and the place of women in it' – Christopher Hill

Man and the Natural World: Changing Attitudes in England 1500–1800 Keith Thomas

'A delight to read and a pleasure to own' – Auberon Waugh in the *Sunday Telegraph*

The Making of the English Working Class E. P. Thompson

Probably the most imaginative – and the most famous – post-war work of English social history.

FOR THE BEST IN PAPERBACKS, LOOK FOR THE

A CHOICE OF PENGUINS AND PELICANS

The French Revolution   Christopher Hibbert

'One of the best accounts of the Revolution that I know . . . Mr Hibbert is outstanding' – J. H. Plumb in the *Sunday Telegraph*

The Germans   Gordon A. Craig

An intimate study of a complex and fascinating nation by 'one of the ablest and most distinguished American historians of modern Germany' – Hugh Trevor-Roper

Ireland: A Positive Proposal   Kevin Boyle and Tom Hadden

A timely and realistic book on Northern Ireland which explains the historical context – and offers a practical and coherent set of proposals which could actually work.

A History of Venice   John Julius Norwich

'Lord Norwich has loved and understood Venice as well as any other Englishman has ever done' – Peter Levi in the *Sunday Times*

Montaillou: Cathars and Catholics in a French Village 1294–1324
Emmanuel Le Roy Ladurie

'A classic adventure in eavesdropping across time' – Michael Ratcliffe in *The Times*

The Defeat of the Spanish Armada   Garrett Mattingly

Published to coincide with the 400th anniversary of the Armada. 'A faultless book; and one which most historians would have given half their working lives to have written' – J. H. Plumb

FOR THE BEST IN PAPERBACKS, LOOK FOR THE

A CHOICE OF PENGUINS AND PELICANS

The Apartheid Handbook   Roger Omond

This book provides the essential hard information about how apartheid actually works from day to day and fills in the details behind the headlines.

The World Turned Upside Down   Christopher Hill

This classic study of radical ideas during the English Revolution 'will stand as a notable monument to . . . one of the finest historians of the present age' – *The Times Literary Supplement*

Islam in the World   Malise Ruthven

'His exposition of "the Qurenic world view" is the most convincing, and the most appealing, that I have read' – Edward Mortimer in *The Times*

The Knight, the Lady and the Priest   Georges Duby

'A very fine book' (Philippe Aries) that traces back to its medieval origin one of our most important institutions, marriage.

A Social History of England   New Edition   Asa Briggs

'A treasure house of scholarly knowledge . . . beautifully written and full of the author's love of his country, its people and its landscape' – John Keegan in the *Sunday Times*, Books of the Year

The Second World War   A J P Taylor

A brilliant and detailed illustrated history, enlivened by all Professor Taylor's customary iconoclasm and wit.

FOR THE BEST IN PAPERBACKS, LOOK FOR THE 🐧

A CHOICE OF PENGUINS AND PELICANS

Adieux   Simone de Beauvoir

This 'farewell to Sartre' by his life-long companion is a 'true labour of love' (the *Listener*) and 'an extraordinary achievement' (*New Statesman*).

British Society 1914–45   John Stevenson

A major contribution to the Pelican Social History of Britain, which 'will undoubtedly be the standard work for students of modern Britain for many years to come' – *The Times Educational Supplement*

The Pelican History of Greek Literature   Peter Levi

A remarkable survey covering all the major writers from Homer to Plutarch, with brilliant translations by the author, one of the leading poets of today.

Art and Literature   Sigmund Freud

Volume 14 of the Pelican Freud Library contains Freud's major essays on Leonardo, Michelangelo and Dostoyevsky, plus shorter pieces on Shakespeare, the nature of creativity and much more.

A History of the Crusades   Sir Steven Runciman

This three-volume history of the events which transferred world power to Western Europe – and founded Modern History – has been universally acclaimed as a masterpiece.

A Night to Remember   Walter Lord

The classic account of the sinking of the *Titanic*. 'A stunning book, incomparably the best on its subject and one of the most exciting books of this or any year' – *The New York Times*

FOR THE BEST IN PAPERBACKS, LOOK FOR THE

A CHOICE OF PENGUINS AND PELICANS

The Informed Heart   Bruno Bettelheim

Bettelheim draws on his experience in concentration camps to illuminate the dangers inherent in all mass societies in this profound and moving masterpiece.

God and the New Physics   Paul Davies

Can science, now come of age, offer a surer path to God than religion? This 'very interesting' (*New Scientist*) book suggests it can.

Modernism   Malcolm Bradbury and James McFarlane (eds.)

A brilliant collection of essays dealing with all aspects of literature and culture for the period 1890–1930 – from Apollinaire and Brecht to Yeats and Zola.

Rise to Globalism   Stephen E. Ambrose

A clear, up-to-date and well-researched history of American foreign policy since 1938, Volume 8 of the Pelican History of the United States.

The Waning of the Middle Ages   Johan Huizinga

A magnificent study of life, thought and art in 14th and 15th century France and the Netherlands, long established as a classic.

The Penguin Dictionary of Psychology   Arthur S. Reber

Over 17,000 terms from psychology, psychiatry and related fields are given clear, concise and modern definitions.

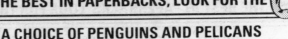

FOR THE BEST IN PAPERBACKS, LOOK FOR THE

A CHOICE OF PENGUINS AND PELICANS

The Literature of the United States Marcus Cunliffe

The fourth edition of a masterly one-volume survey, described by D. W. Brogan in the *Guardian* as 'a very good book indeed'.

The Sceptical Feminist Janet Radcliffe Richards

A rigorously argued but sympathetic consideration of feminist claims. 'A triumph' – *Sunday Times*

The Enlightenment Norman Hampson

A classic survey of the age of Diderot and Voltaire, Goethe and Hume, which forms part of the Pelican History of European Thought.

Defoe to the Victorians David Skilton

'Learned and stimulating' (*The Times Educational Supplement*). A fascinating survey of two centuries of the English novel.

Reformation to Industrial Revolution Christopher Hill

This 'formidable little book' (Peter Laslett in the *Guardian*) by one of our leading historians is Volume 2 of the Pelican Economic History of Britain.

The New Pelican Guide to English Literature Boris Ford (ed.)
Volume 8: The Present

This book brings a major series up to date with important essays on Ted Hughes and Nadine Gordimer, Philip Larkin and V. S. Naipaul, and all the other leading writers of today.

FOR THE BEST IN PAPERBACKS, LOOK FOR THE

A CHOICE OF PENGUINS AND PELICANS

A Question of Economics   Peter Donaldson

Twenty key issues – the City, trade unions, 'free market forces' and many others – are presented clearly and fully in this major book based on a television series.

The Economist Economics   Rupert Pennant-Rea and Clive Crook

Based on a series of 'briefs' published in the *Economist* in 1984, this important new book makes the key issues of contemporary economic thinking accessible to the general reader.

The Tyranny of the Status Quo   Milton and Rose Friedman

Despite the rhetoric, big government has actually *grown* under Reagan and Thatcher. The Friedmans consider why this is – and what we can do now to change it.

Business Wargames   Barrie G. James

Successful companies use military strategy to win. Barrie James shows how – and draws some vital lessons for today's manager.

Atlas of Management Thinking   Edward de Bono

This fascinating book provides a vital repertoire of non-verbal images – to help activate the right side of any manager's brain.

The Winning Streak   Walter Goldsmith and David Clutterbuck

_____ of what Britain's best-run and successful companies